Alix Paré

CATS IN ART

FROM PREHISTORIC TO
NEO-POP MASTERPIECES

T tra.publishing

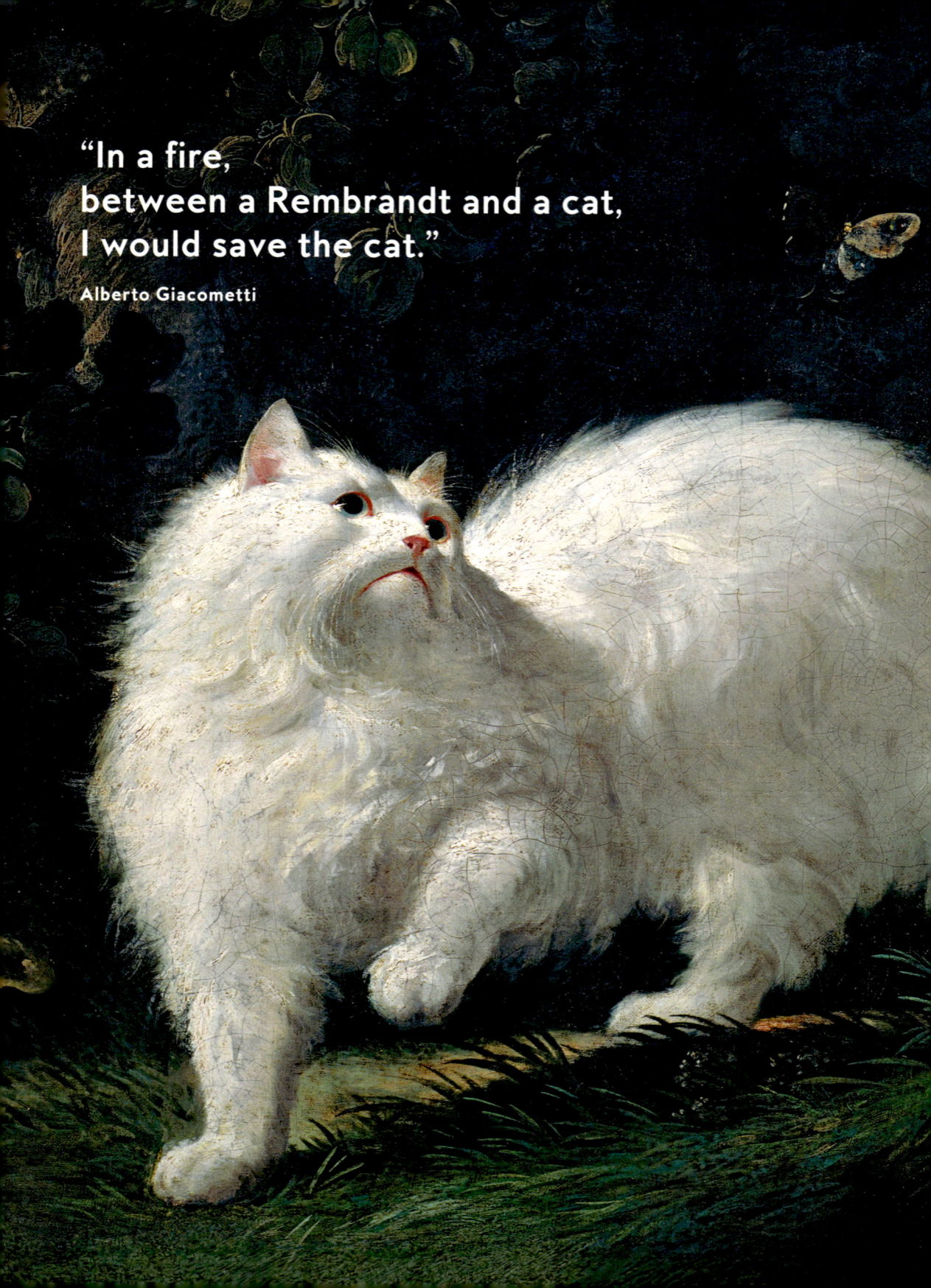

"In a fire,
between a Rembrandt and a cat,
I would save the cat."

Alberto Giacometti

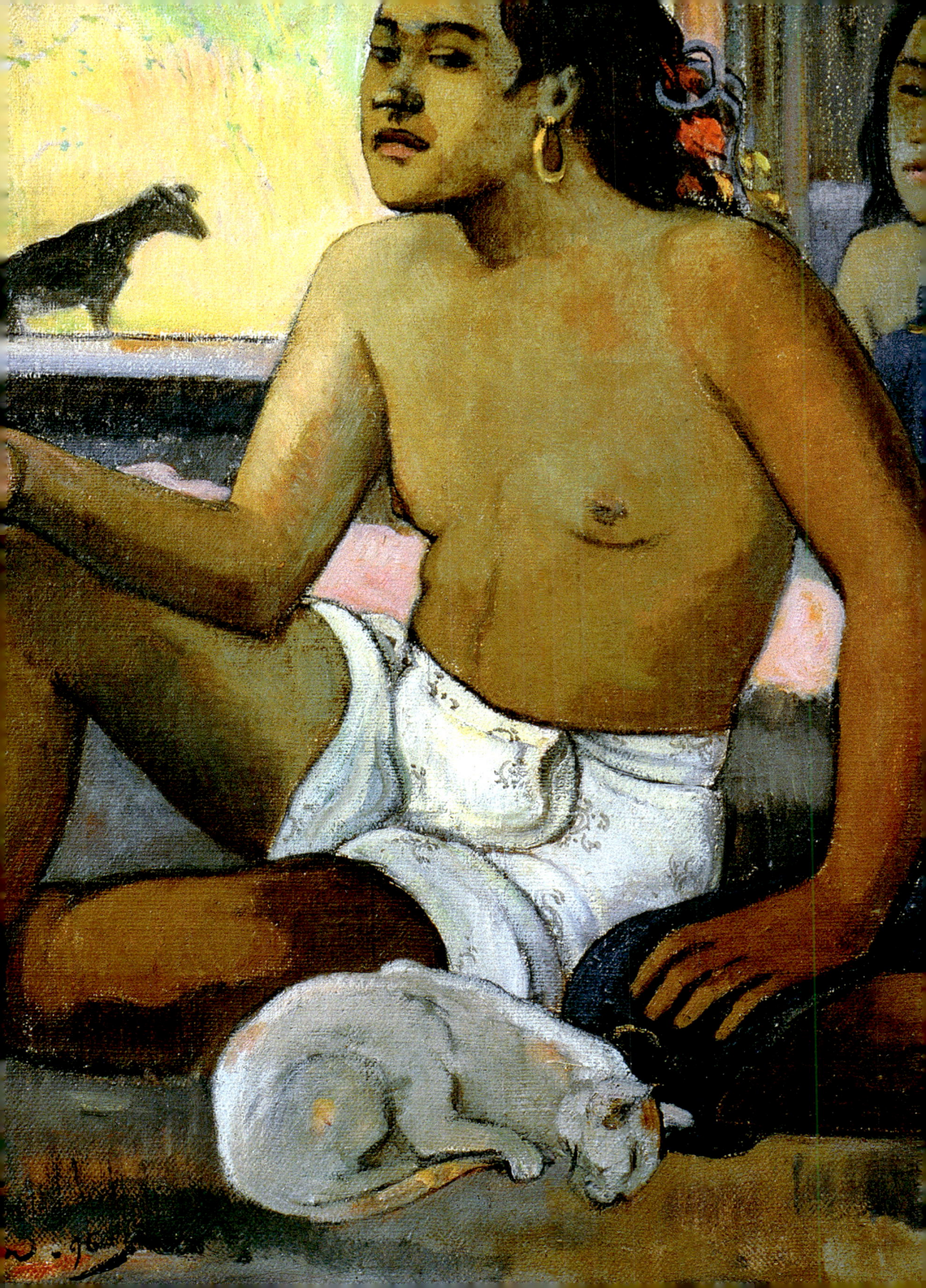

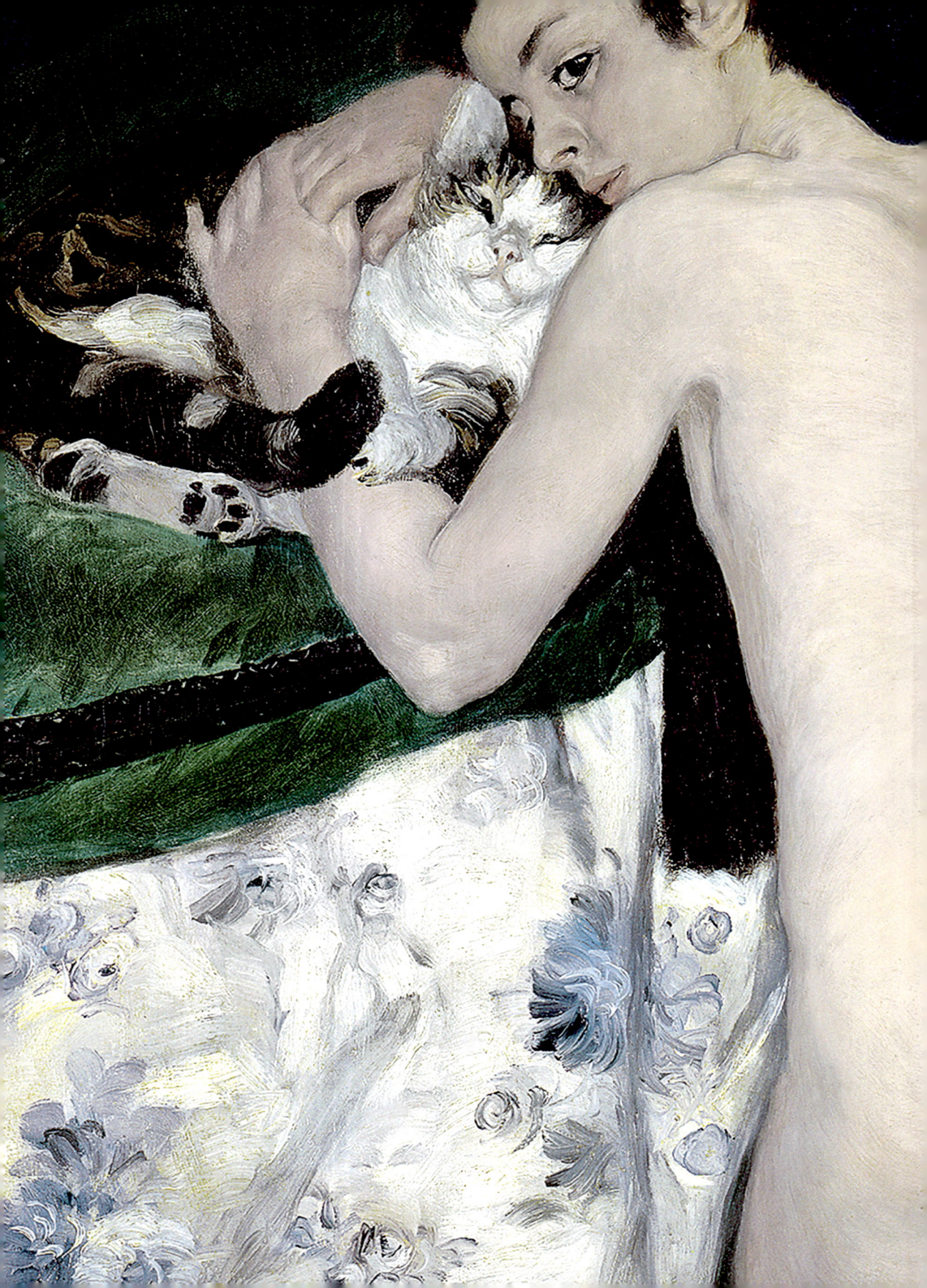

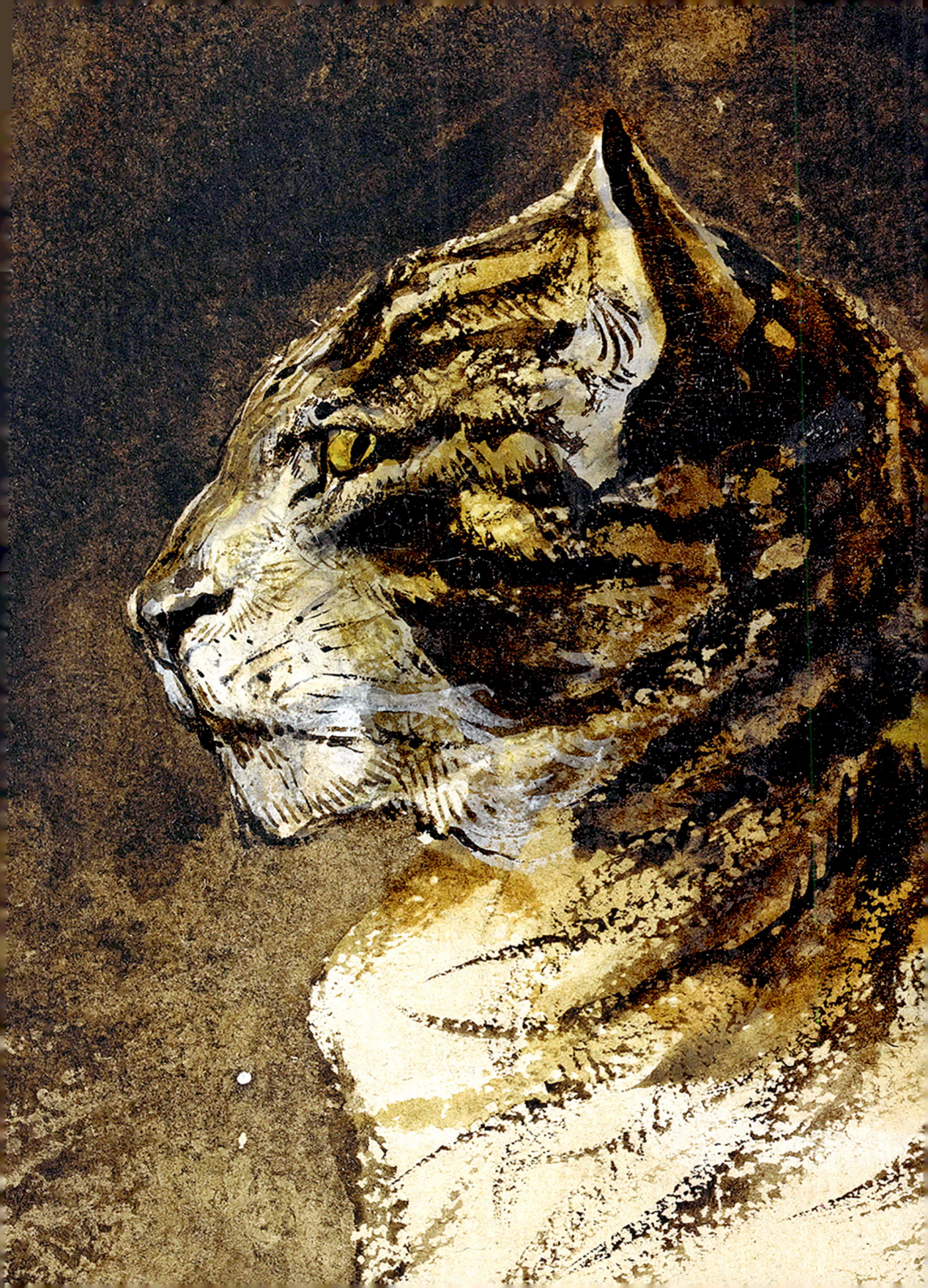

Cats in Art

From Wildcat to Lap Cat

The cat is the world's most beloved pet, ahead of the dog. Yet the relationship between man and cat wasn't always so radiant! What do works of art tell us about our shared history with cats?

Divine Feline

Our cohabitation with cats is nothing new. It dates back to Neolithic times and coincides with the development of agriculture. Grain stocks in villages lead to the arrival of rodents and their natural predator: the cat. For sanitary reasons, it is in the interest of humans to let the feline into their homes. The animal is gradually tamed, but not really domesticated. Archaeological evidence attests to this ancient cohabitation in the Mediterranean basin. In Egypt, cats hunt rodents, scorpions, and snakes. Its beneficial presence makes it a revered animal. From the 1st millennium BCE, cats are associated with the goddess Bastet. Cat statuettes and mummies are produced in abundance.

In Search of Recognition

In Europe, from antiquity to the end of the Middle Ages, the cat is almost absent from works of art. This half-domestic, half-wild animal, which seems to have a strong link with the mysteries of nature, is mistrusted. The cat takes on all sorts of negative connotations: it is the animal of laziness, cruelty, gluttony, sensuality, and even lust. It is often associated with the Devil and witches. The cat's presence in art progresses along with its acceptance by mankind. In the space of a few centuries, it goes from being a mere detail in the margin of a manuscript to becoming a veritable subject for painters.

Insubmissive

The independence of cats is well known. **Buffon**, in his *Histoire Naturelle*, already points this out: "It cannot be said that cats, though living in our houses, are entirely domestic. The most familiar are not under any subjection, but rather enjoy perfect freedom, as they only do just what they please."

To the Stake!

Until the Renaissance, it is rare to come across cats in religious art, even in paintings of **Noah's Ark**. For centuries, Christianity associates the feline with the Devil and heretics. The **Inquisition** orders the sacrifice of cats during popular festivals. A practice that continues until the end of the 18th century in eastern France.

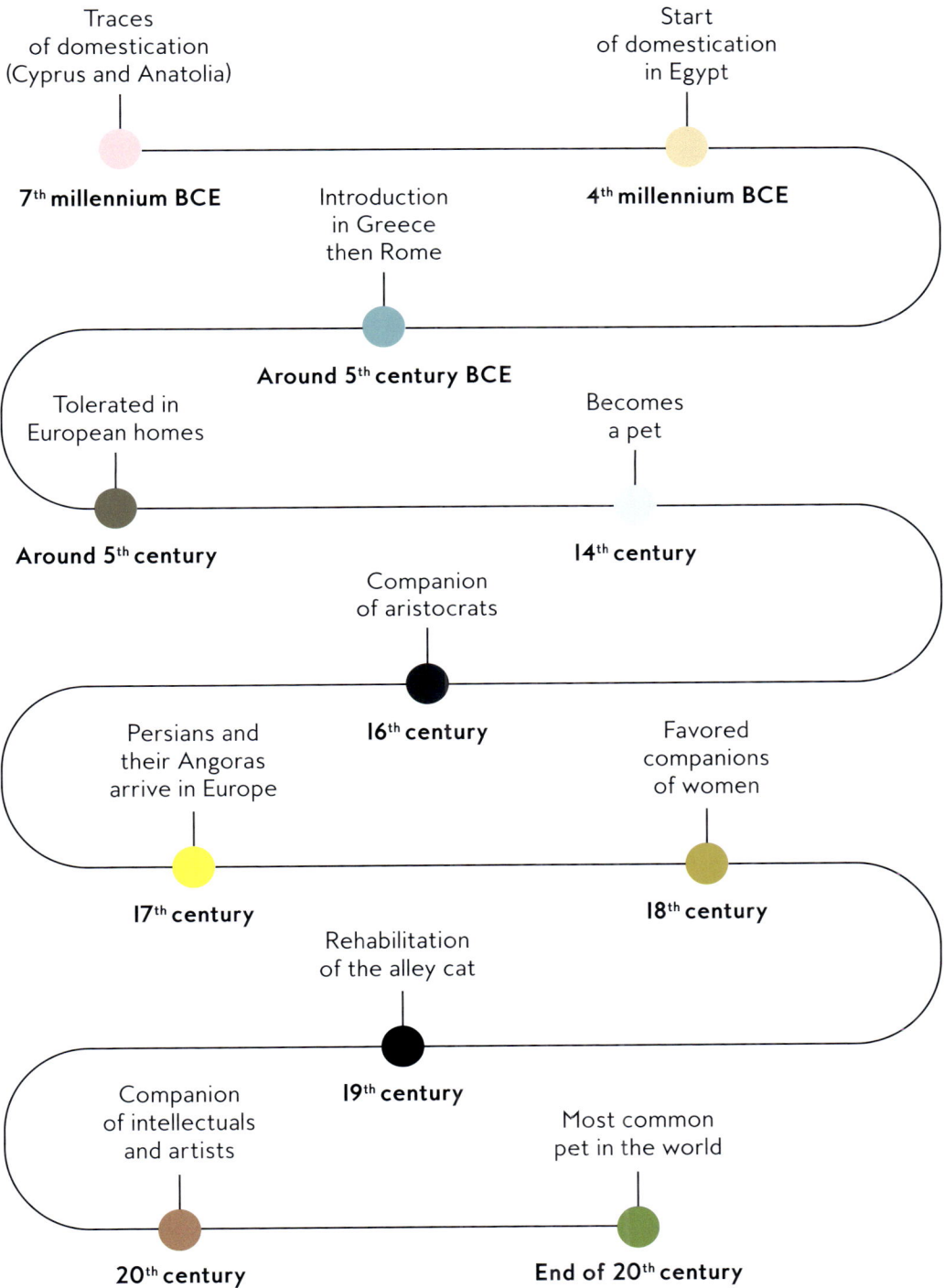

Traces
of domestication
(Cyprus and Anatolia)

7th millennium BCE

Start
of domestication
in Egypt

4th millennium BCE

Introduction
in Greece
then Rome

Around 5th century BCE

Tolerated in
European homes

Around 5th century

Becomes
a pet

14th century

Companion
of aristocrats

16th century

Persians and
their Angoras
arrive in Europe

17th century

Favored
companions
of women

18th century

Rehabilitation
of the alley cat

19th century

Companion
of intellectuals
and artists

20th century

Most common
pet in the world

End of 20th century

"The cat became a great lord,
and never again ran after mice, except for entertainment."

Charles Perrault, *The Master Cat or Puss in Boots*

Cat vs. Dog

There are an estimated **four hundred million cats** in the world. Since the 1990s, the number of cats has exceeded the number of dogs in the West. Better suited to apartment living, cuddly but independent... the tomcat is more appreciated.

And in Asia?

The cat is introduced to **China** in the early **Han** dynasty, through trade. The cat becomes a pet with positive symbolism. It arrives in **Japan** around the 6th century, at the same time as **Buddhism**. We know that in 999, **Emperor Ichijō** receives one as a gift for his birthday.

Various Sign Projects Topped with Black Cats
(*Divers Projets Denseignes Surmontées De Chats Noirs*)
Théophile Alexandre Steinlen
1896
Indian ink wash and graphite
Musée d'Orsay, Paris
(Preserved in the Musée du Louvre)

Artists' Muse

From the Renaissance onwards, the tomcat becomes the friend of poets and artists, and even wins the admiration of Leonardo da Vinci. The arrival of exotic cats, Angoras and Persians, helps to soften its image. From the Renaissance to the 18th century, the alley cat makes its debut in religious paintings, still lifes, scenes of daily life, and then, with immense success, in portraiture. In the 19th century, painters identify more than ever with the alley cat, which they are helping to rehabilitate. They like to depict this mysterious, solitary, nocturnal companion vagabond. From Delacroix to Gauguin, via Manet, Renoir, or Vallotton, all the great artists rub shoulders with a feline theme. Cats invade paintings, sculptures, engravings, posters, and trinkets. And literature is not left out: Baudelaire, Maupassant, Pierre Loti . . . Who doesn't like cats?

A Pampered Model

The 20th century establishes the cat as the indoor pet par excellence. Friends of writers and artists, they sleep on their masters' desks or in their studios. The cats of Bonnard, Matisse, Foujita, Balthus, and Warhol appear in their paintings. The cats of the greatest photographers are not left out. The big eyes and curves of the feline are particularly captivating. The tomcat also becomes a hero of children's literature and a star of comics and the Internet. Today, it seems to have lost its negative connotations, except perhaps for those who dread coming across a black cat.

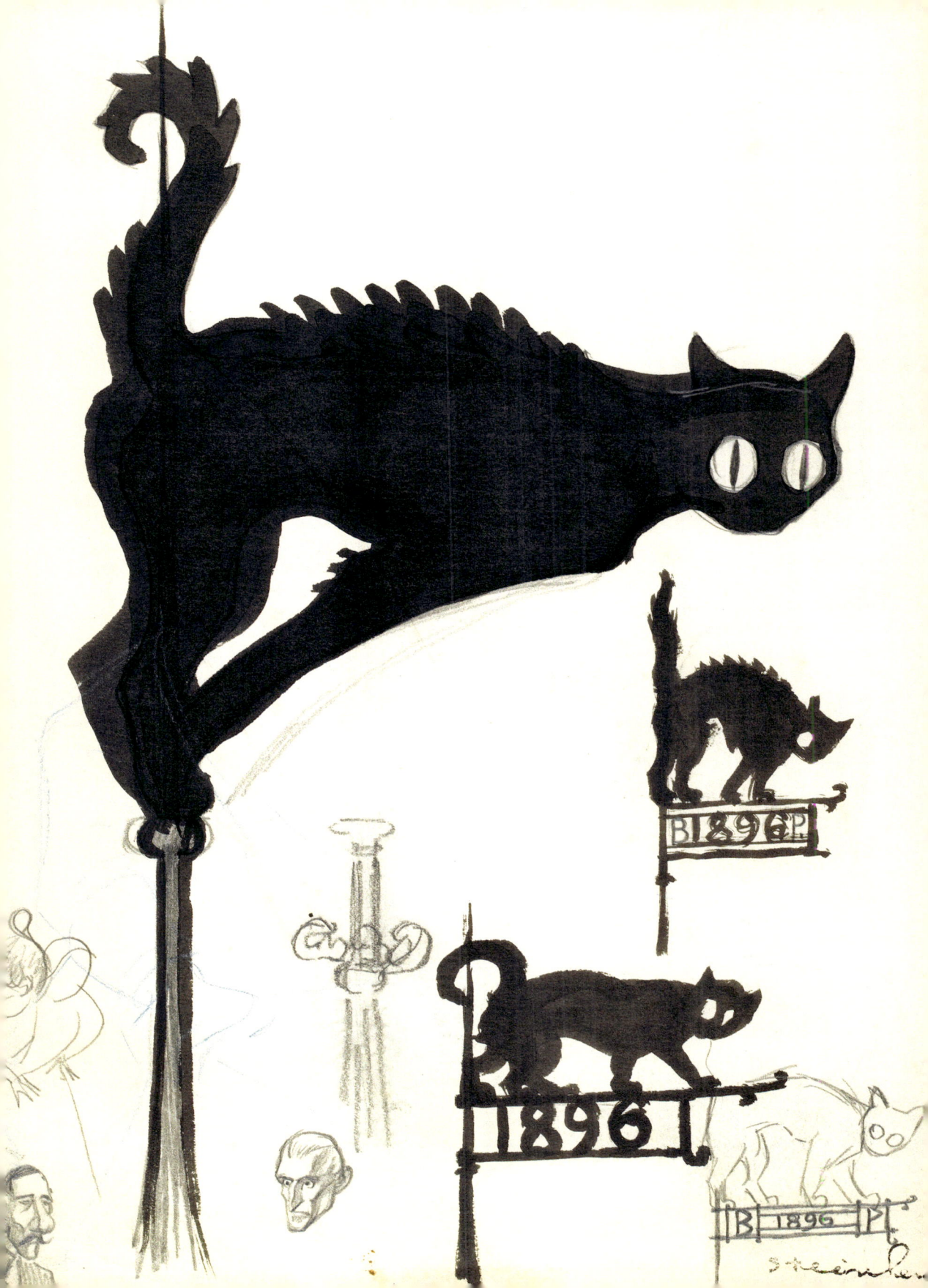

Geographical Landmarks

The Cat Conquering the World

A Progressive Domestication

- 🟡 Neolithic

- 🟠 Antiquity

- 🔵 From the beginning of the Common Era to the 15th century

- 🔵 After 1500

- 🐾 First traces of domestication
  7th millennium BCE

- 🐱 Domestication and divinization
  4th millennium BCE

Species or Race?

The cat, *Felis silvestris catus*, is a domesticated subspecies of the wildcat, a feline that has largely disappeared in Europe but is still widespread in Asia and Africa. There are some fifty breeds of domestic cat.

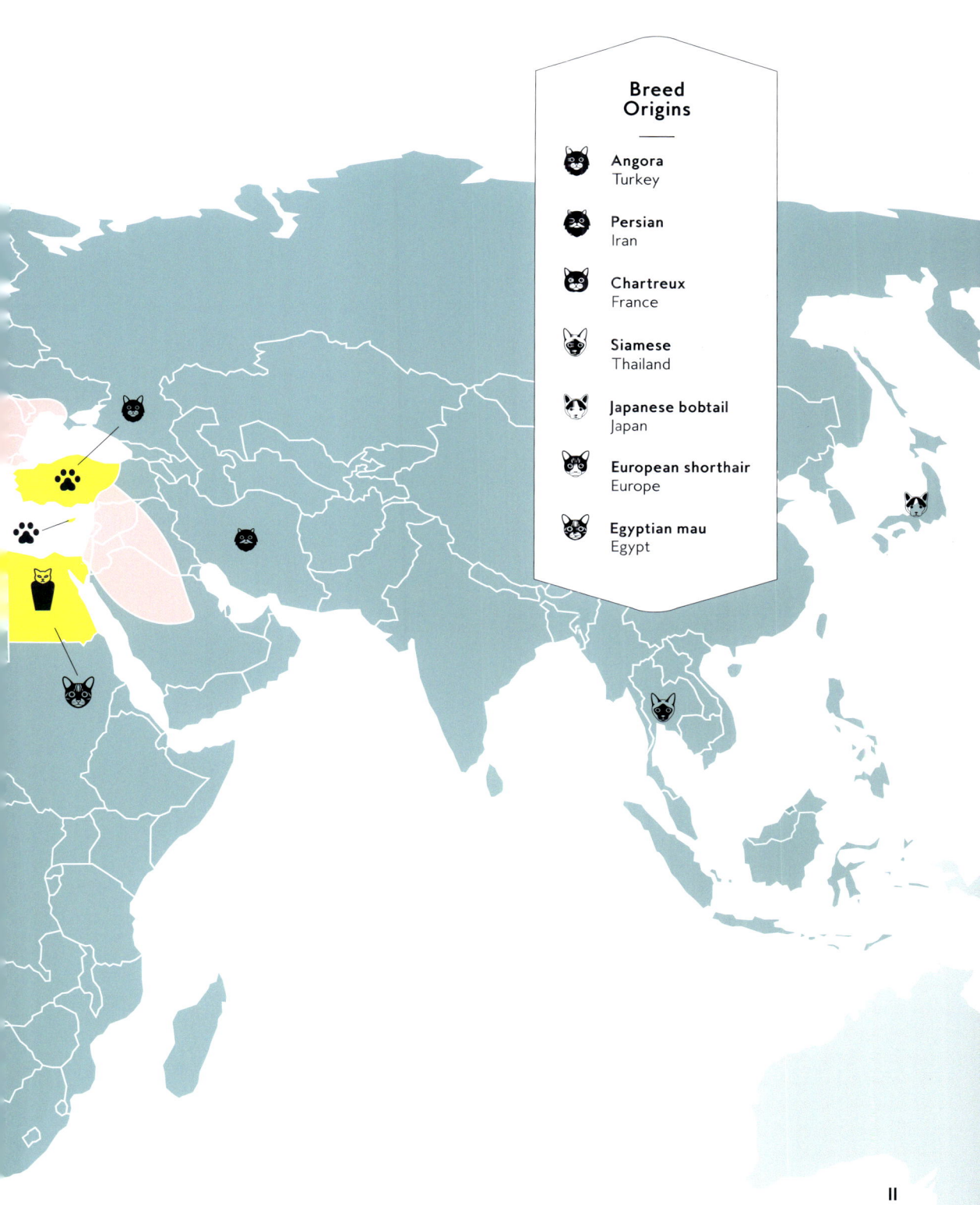

Breed Origins

Angora
Turkey

Persian
Iran

Chartreux
France

Siamese
Thailand

Japanese bobtail
Japan

European shorthair
Europe

Egyptian mau
Egypt

Words and Cats

Divine or Demonic?

Since the 13th century and the *Roman de Renart*, the cat has been the literary animal par excellence—the hero of tales, legends, novels, and poems. It is also a friend to writers who like to describe the thousand facets of its personality.

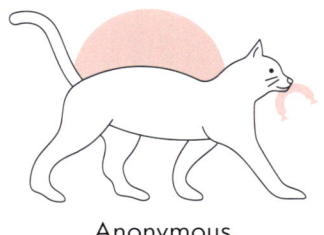

Anonymous,
Le Roman de Renart

Books Featuring Cats

Around 1200

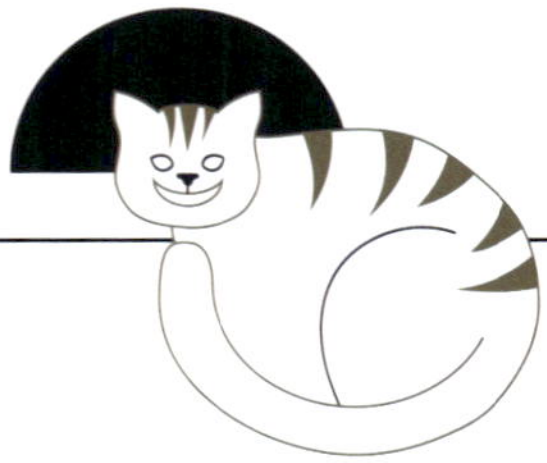

Countess of Ségur,
Blondine

1856

Lewis Carroll,
Alice in Wonderland

Émile Zola,
"The Paradise of Cats"

1865

1874

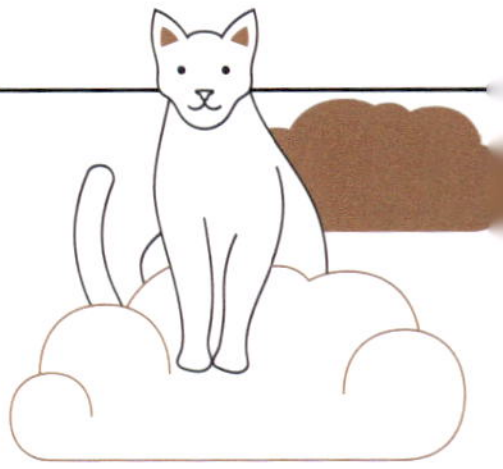

Boris Vian,
"Blues for a Black Cat"

1949

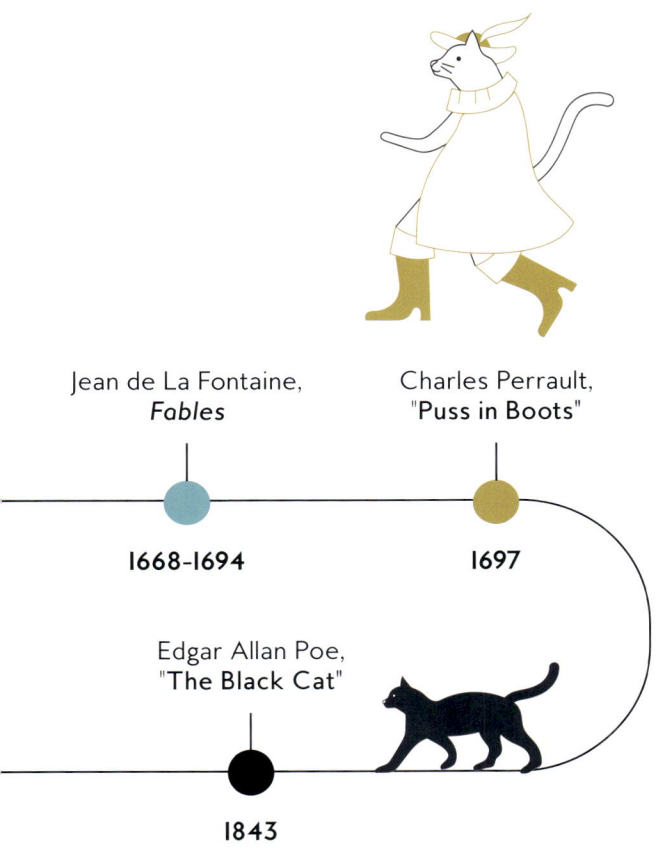

Jean de La Fontaine,
Fables

1668-1694

Charles Perrault,
"Puss in Boots"

1697

Edgar Allan Poe,
"The Black Cat"

1843

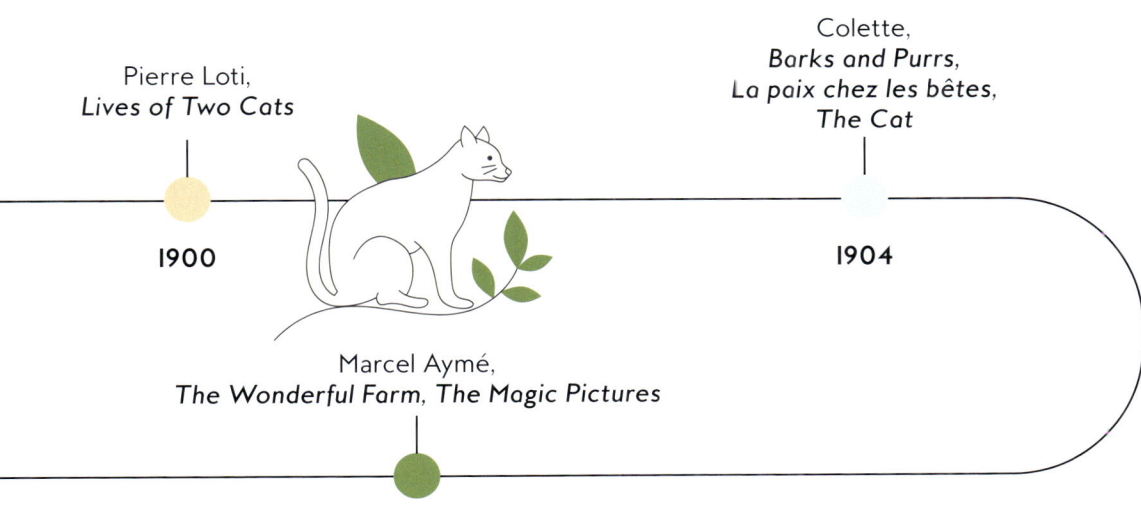

Pierre Loti,
Lives of Two Cats

1900

Colette,
*Barks and Purrs,
La paix chez les bêtes,
The Cat*

1904

Marcel Aymé,
The Wonderful Farm, The Magic Pictures

1946

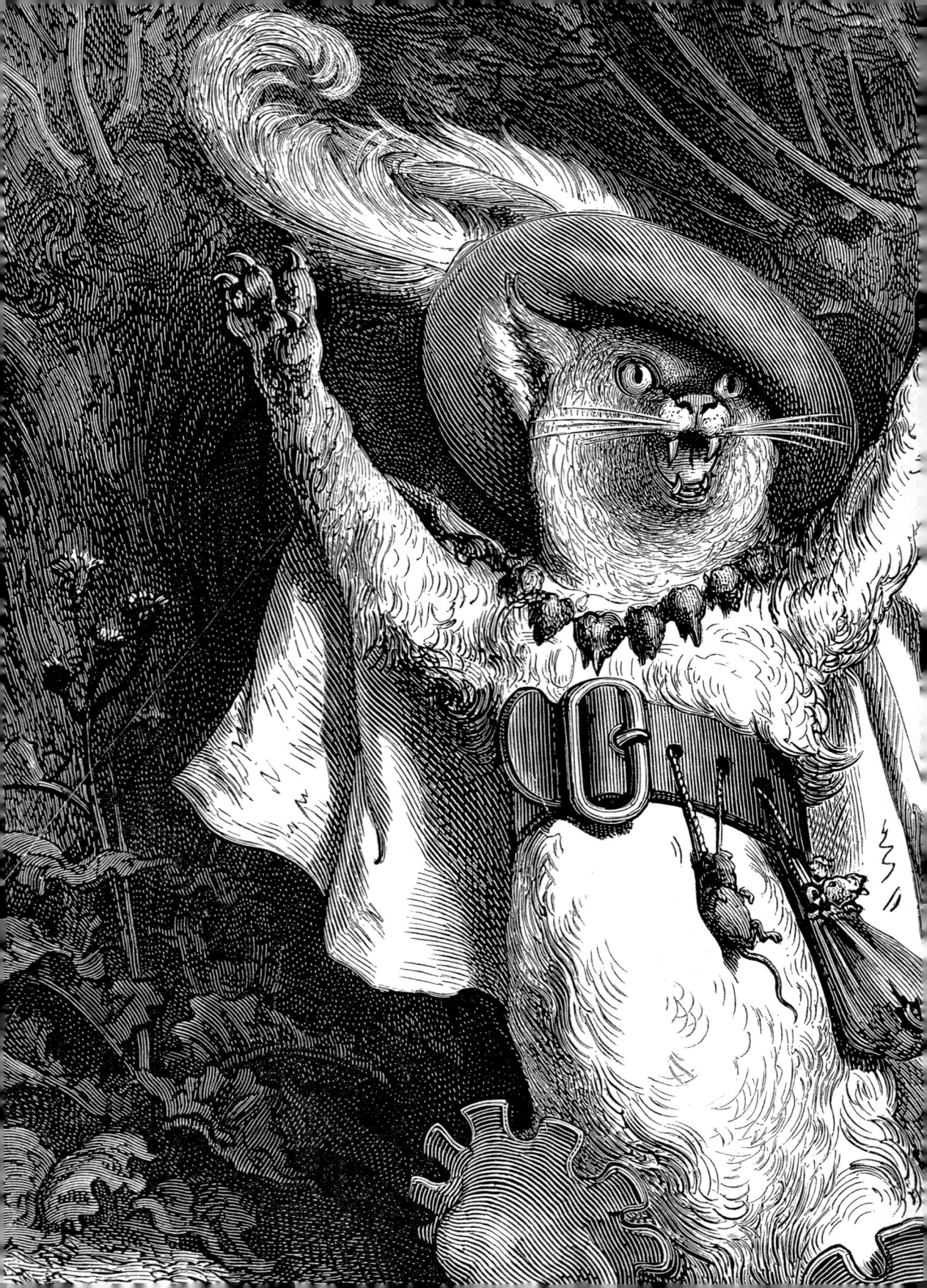

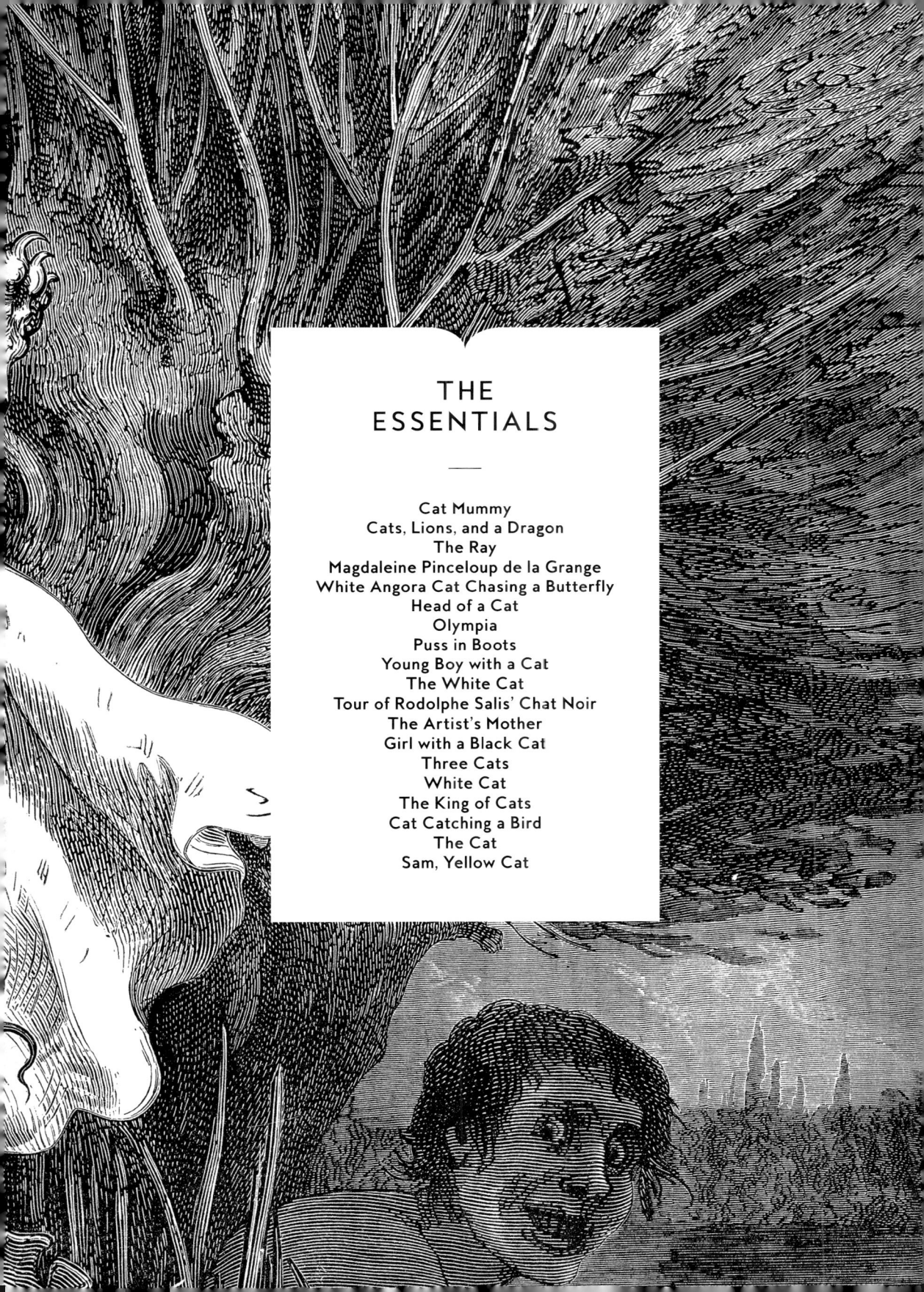

THE ESSENTIALS

—

Cat Mummy

7th century BCE

Animal Mummies

Other animal mummies are offered to Egyptian divinities: **dogs** to the god Anubis, **ibises** or **monkeys** to the god Thoth, but also **crocodiles**—they are used to ask for mercy, as a token of thanks, or to ensure the donor an eternal link with the divinity.

Gods in their Animal Forms

Ram: Khnum, Amun
Cat: Hathor, Bastet
Dog: Anubis
Crocodile: Sebek
Falcon: Horus, Re, Montu, Khonsu
Hippopotamus: Taouret
Ibis: Thoth
Scarab: Khepri
Serpent (Cobra): Apophis, Ouadjet, Renenutet
Monkey (Baboon): Thoth
Cow: Isis, Hathor
Vulture: Mout, Nekhbet

History of Mummification

The cat is an emblem of Egyptian art, featured on statues, mummies, tomb paintings, and much more. It is often associated with Bastet, the goddess of the Home and Maternity, the protector of pregnant women and children.

Animal worship in Egypt dates back to the 4th millennium BCE, but it takes on increasing importance at the end of the Pharaonic period and until Roman domination, also known as the Late Period (7th to 4th century BCE). The cat mummy dates back to this Late Period.

Bastet has not always been associated with the cat. The Egyptian gods don't have a clearly defined identity, but an infinite number of names and forms. First associated with Hathor, the cat doesn't lend its features to Bastet until 1000 or 800 BCE. Before that, she is a woman or lioness. She eventually becomes a gentle feline, attentive to her kittens, who often cling to her teats.

There are countless cat mummies deposited in the Bastet sanctuaries. Acquiring a cat mummy was not complicated and much less expensive than an elegant bronze statuette. Animals were specially bred by priests to be killed and mummified. The mummies were then sold to pilgrims and buried in necropolises. The most famous Bastet sanctuary is that of Bubastis.

Scientific imaging has revealed that cats were killed very young—spine broken, skull caved in—but also that some mummies actually contain very few, if any, animal remains! The quality and "filling" of mummies vary according to the means of the purchaser. The texts even speak of "cat buriers."

Cat Mummy
(Momie de chat)
7th century BCE
Musée du Louvre, Paris

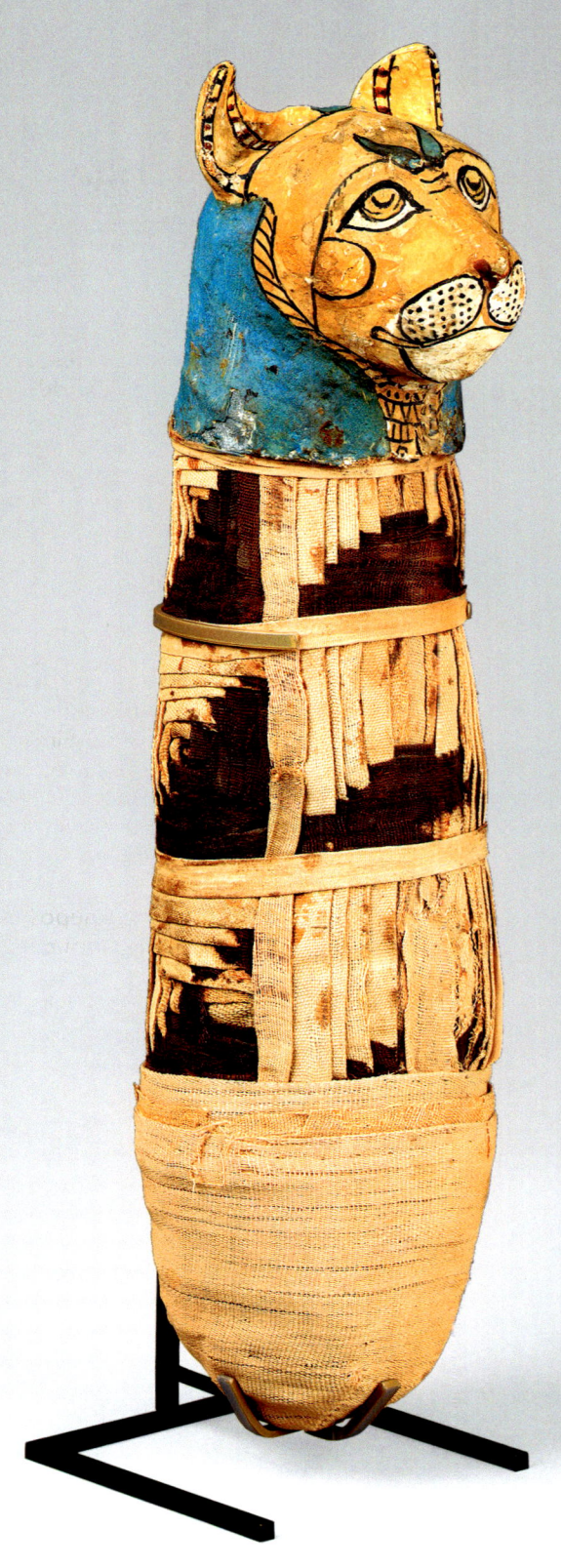

Cats, Lions, and a Dragon

1517-1518

Jesus and His Cat

In the early 1480s, **da Vinci** produces several drawings on the theme of the **Virgin and Child** with a cat. The infant Jesus embraces the animal, which is trying to escape. Is the feline a symbol of evil? No corresponding painting has ever been found.

Da Vinci Said

"Even the smallest of felines, the cat, is a masterpiece."

Feline Projects

More than his paintings, Leonardo da Vinci's manuscripts attest to the variety and profusion of subjects that interest him. Cats are no exception.

Da Vinci draws some twenty little cats in brown ink. The felines are shown in a variety of attitudes: sleeping, licking, stretching, watching, and fighting. Body volume, muscles, furs, and facial expressions are rendered with great precision. Other cats, in action, are the result of observation and memory.

In this work, a few sketches of lions and a dragon mingle with the cats. The coherence between these three animals, real or imaginary, is explained by da Vinci himself at the bottom of the page: "Of flexion and extension. The lion is the prince of this animal species, because of the flexibility of its spine . . ." The artist often links written reflections to his drawings. It's not question of preparatory sketching but rather of scientific research. The scholar is interested in flexibility and torsion.

Between art and science, da Vinci is interested in everything. His analytical mind is coupled with an extraordinary thirst for knowledge. Around 1513-1514, in the margin of a treatise he had begun on human anatomy, he mentions the project of another treatise, on animal movement: "Write a separate treatise describing the movements of animals with four feet, among which is man, who likewise in his infancy crawls on all fours." Our cats—along with another similar page depicting a cat, horses, and dragons—are perhaps drafts of this project. The two pages are dated 1517 or 1518, a year before the artist's death, at the height of his fame. Established in France, da Vinci became painter, engineer, and architect to King Francis I.

Cats, Lions, and a Dragon
Leonardo da Vinci
1517-1518
Black chalk, pen and ink, wash
Royal Library, Windsor

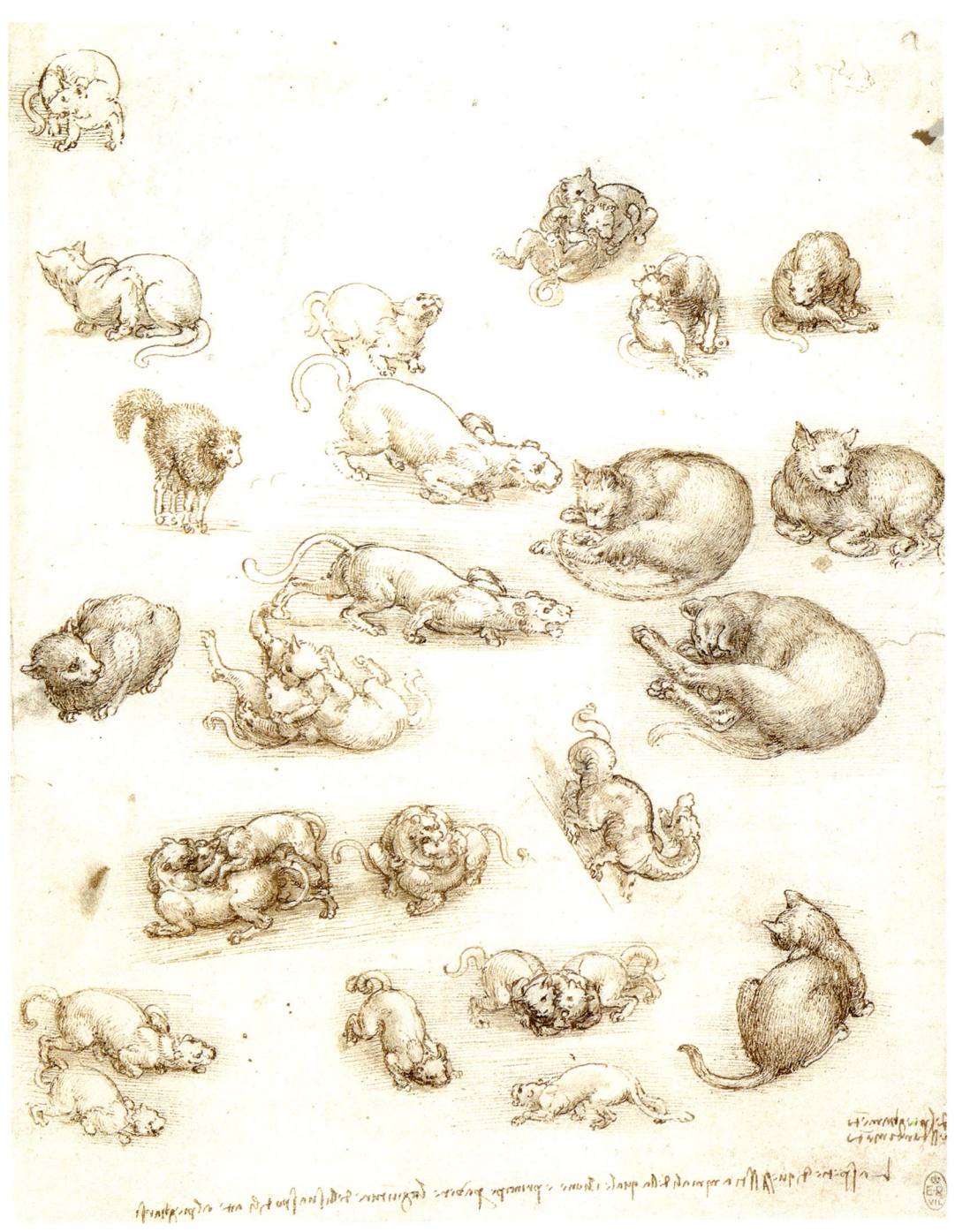

The Ray

Around 1725–1726

The Cat and the Monster

Here's a still life that's not quite a still life. A lively cat stands next to the hanging stingray. This astonishing painting is considered a masterpiece, fascinating Diderot, Proust, Matisse, and Soutine.

In a stone niche, an eviscerated ray hangs from a hook. It's a female; the pouch containing the egg has been preserved. The fish's nostrils and mouth form a strange face, at once hypnotic and repulsive. To the right of the ray, the world of objects: a stoneware pitcher, a bottle of wine, a saucepan, a cauldron, a skimmer, and a knife. On the left, the organic world: two dead barbels, oysters, small leeks, and an alley cat with a spotted snout.

Our feline's taste buds are on fire. So as not to slip, it steps carefully over the oysters. Its eyes are fixed on the two fish in the center of the table. Its body is arched, its tail raised, its ears pricked. Thanks to the cat, Chardin introduces suspense into what could have been a simple still life. It also exalts the five senses: trying to make as little noise as possible, the cat looks at and sniffs what it wants to touch and taste.

Thanks to this simple yet highly mastered composition, Chardin surprises and enchants the greatest painters of his time, who admire not only the construction of the image, but also the striking rendering of materials, the shiny, wet look of the fish. Chardin is just twenty-eight. He is a young, unknown artist, and the exhibition of this painting at the Royal Academy of Painting and Sculpture earns him approval and acceptance the same day. This is quite exceptional when you consider that, for some artists, it can take up to three years!

The Royal Academy

During the childhood of **King Louis XIV**, the Royal Academy of Painting and Sculpture is created in Paris. This state organization is responsible for training the kingdom's artists. The practice and theories of art and good taste are taught there. Closed after the Revolution, the Academy is reborn in 1817 as the **École des Beaux-Arts**, which still exists today.

A Timeless Model

Diderot considers *The Ray* to be a masterpiece that every young painter should copy. **Matisse** confides that it was one of the works he studied most when visiting the Louvre, and **Soutine** proposes an expressionist homage to it in 1924. As for **Marcel Proust**, he writes a remarkable description of the painting in "Chardin and Rembrandt."

"The eye, which loves to play with the other senses [...] can already sense the freshness of the oysters that will wet the cat's paws."

Marcel Proust

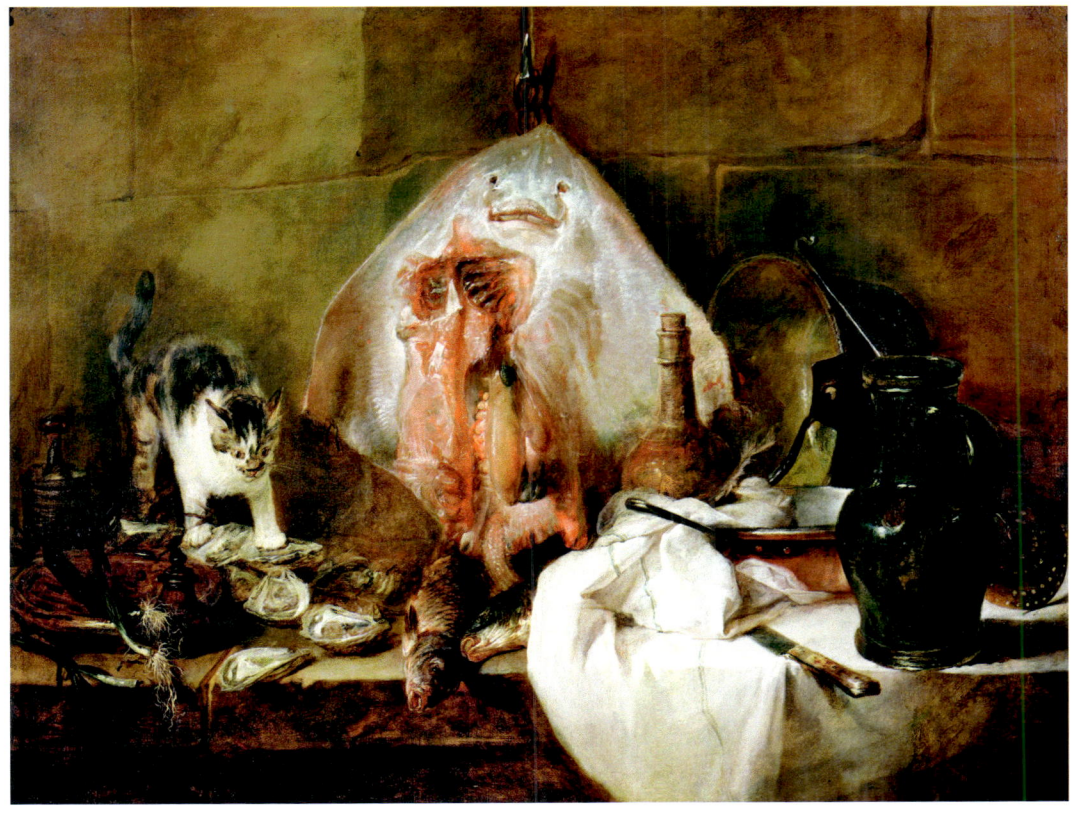

The Ray
(La Raie)
Jean Siméon Chardin
1725-1726
Oil on canvas
Musée du Louvre, Paris

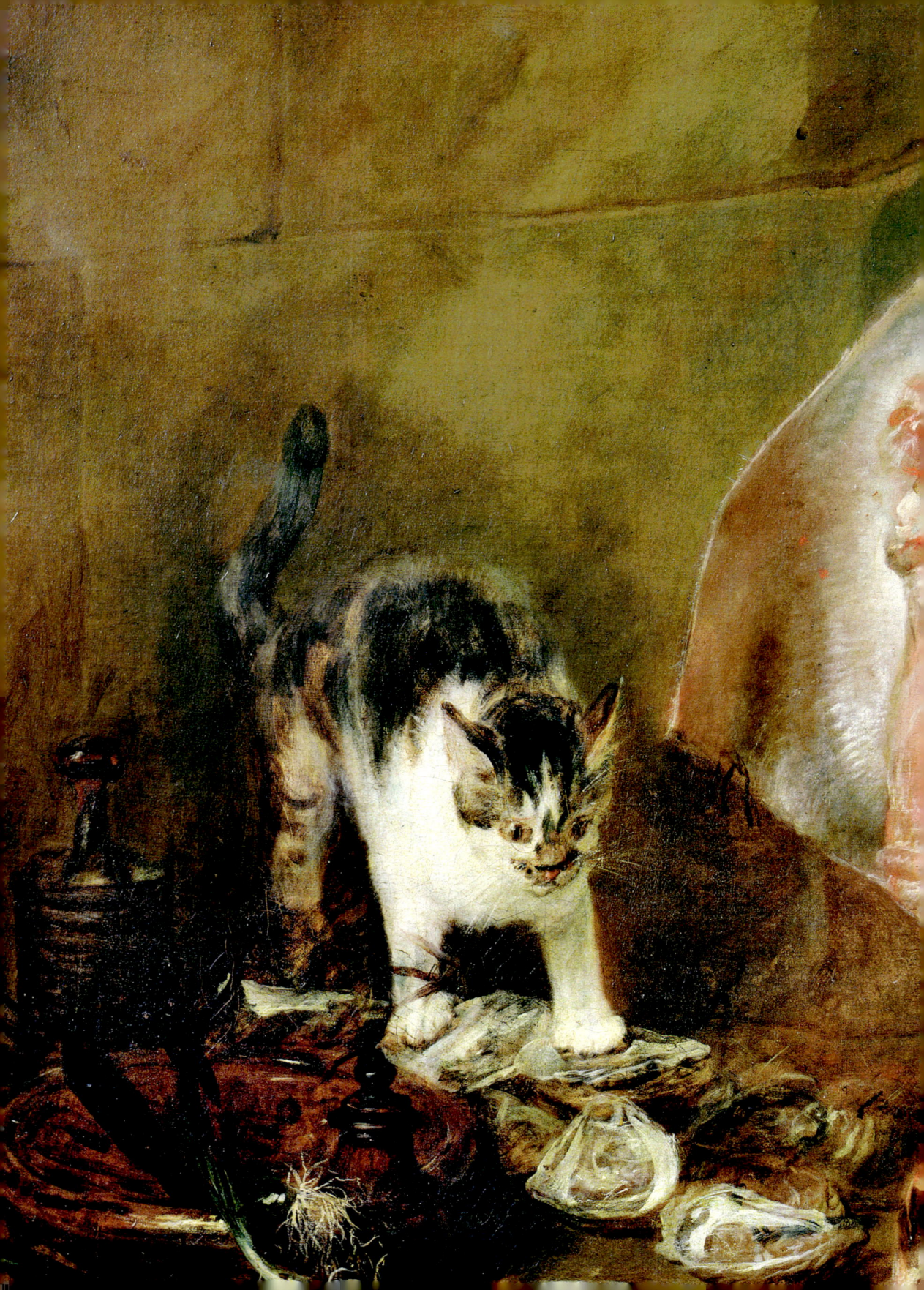

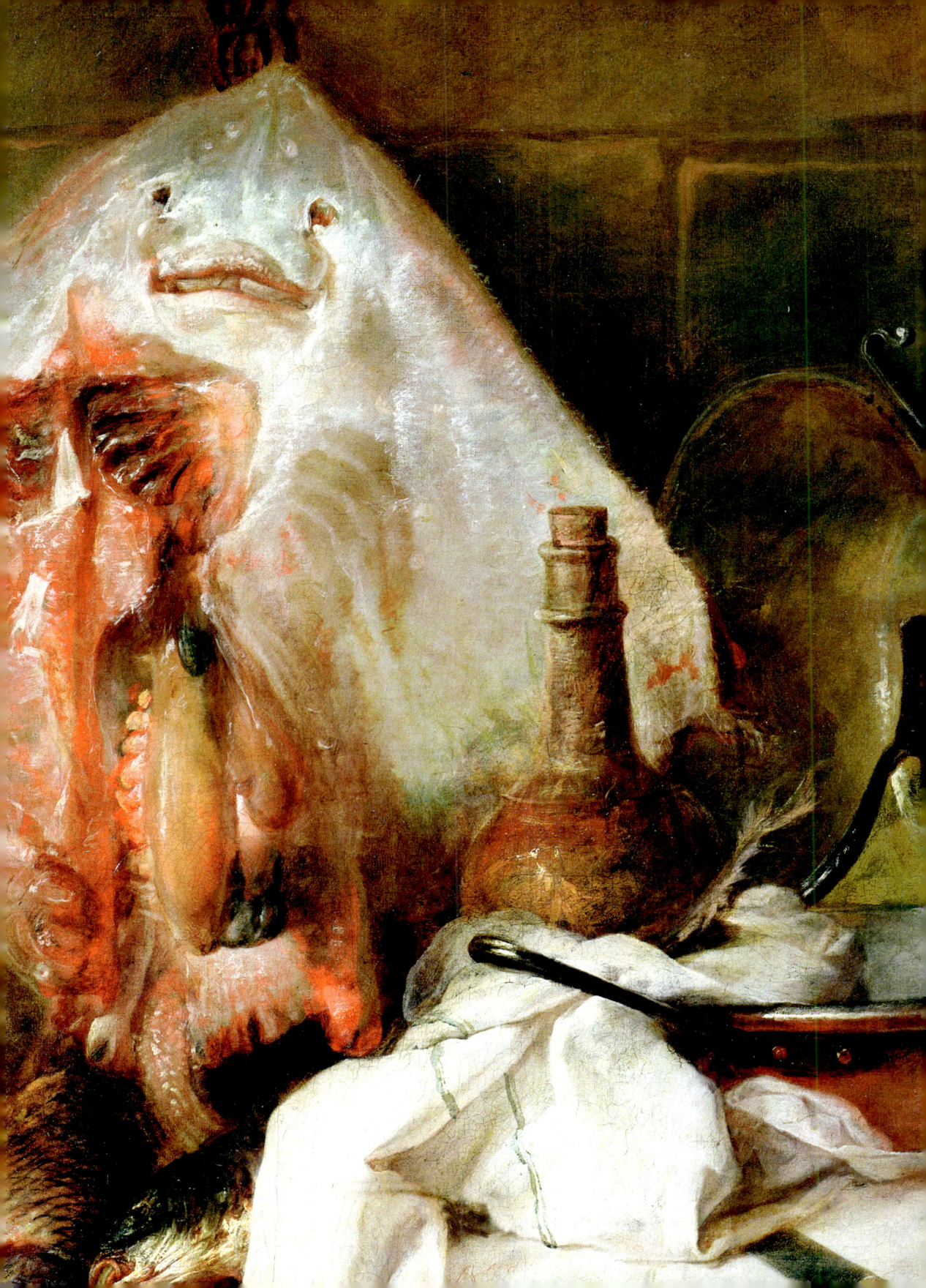

Magdaleine Pinceloup de la Grange

1747

KEY FIGURES
Women and Girls with Cats

Theodore Gericault, *Portrait of Louise Vernet as a Child* — 1818

1880 — Edouard Manet, *Woman with a Cat*

Pierre Auguste Renoir, *Julie Manet* — 1887

1912 — Pierre Bonnard, *Woman with a Cat*

Fernand Léger, *Woman with a Cat* — 1921

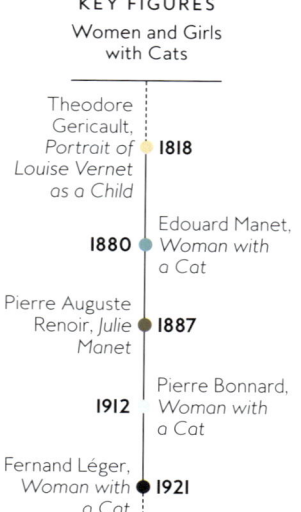

Magdaleine Pinceloup de la Grange
Jean-Baptiste Perronneau
1747
Oil on canvas
J. Paul Getty Museum, Los Angeles

Luxury Companion

Charles François Pinceloup de la Grange is an officer and advisor to Louis XV. Proud of his rise, he commissions Jean-Baptiste Perronneau to paint a portrait of himself and one of his wife, Magdaleine.

Madame Pinceloup de la Grange doesn't look very comfortable. Rather stiff, she sits in profile on a chair, lifts her chin, and turns her head slightly. She looks into the distance, but in her arms, her Chartreux calls out to us.

At the time, this ancient breed of cat with its velvety gray coat is one of the most expensive. In the 18th century, these noble cats are praised for their beauty by the naturalist Buffon in his *Histoire Naturelle*. The silky gray coat of Magdaleine's cat is a perfect match to her fashionable hairstyle, expertly curled and lightly powdered. It wears a necklace of golden bells, echoing the pearls on its mistress's choker. This cat isn't just a pet, but a fashion accessory!

Perronneau includes several cats in his portraits of women or young girls (*Mademoiselle Huquier, A Girl with a Kitten*). More than personal taste, it's a social phenomenon. In the 18th century, the cat became the favored pet of women and children. In the arms of little girls, it evokes gentleness and delicacy. Associated with women, it evokes the elegance and comfort of living rooms, if not a certain eroticism. Note that the alley cat is still well-loved in working-class circles.

Some aristocrats are so attached to their tomcats that they commission marble tombs engraved with tearful eulogies. The Duchess of Lesdiguières had a monument to Ménine erected in her garden, "of all cats the most lovely and most beloved." On a black marble sarcophagus, a sculpted Ménine sits on a white marble cushion.

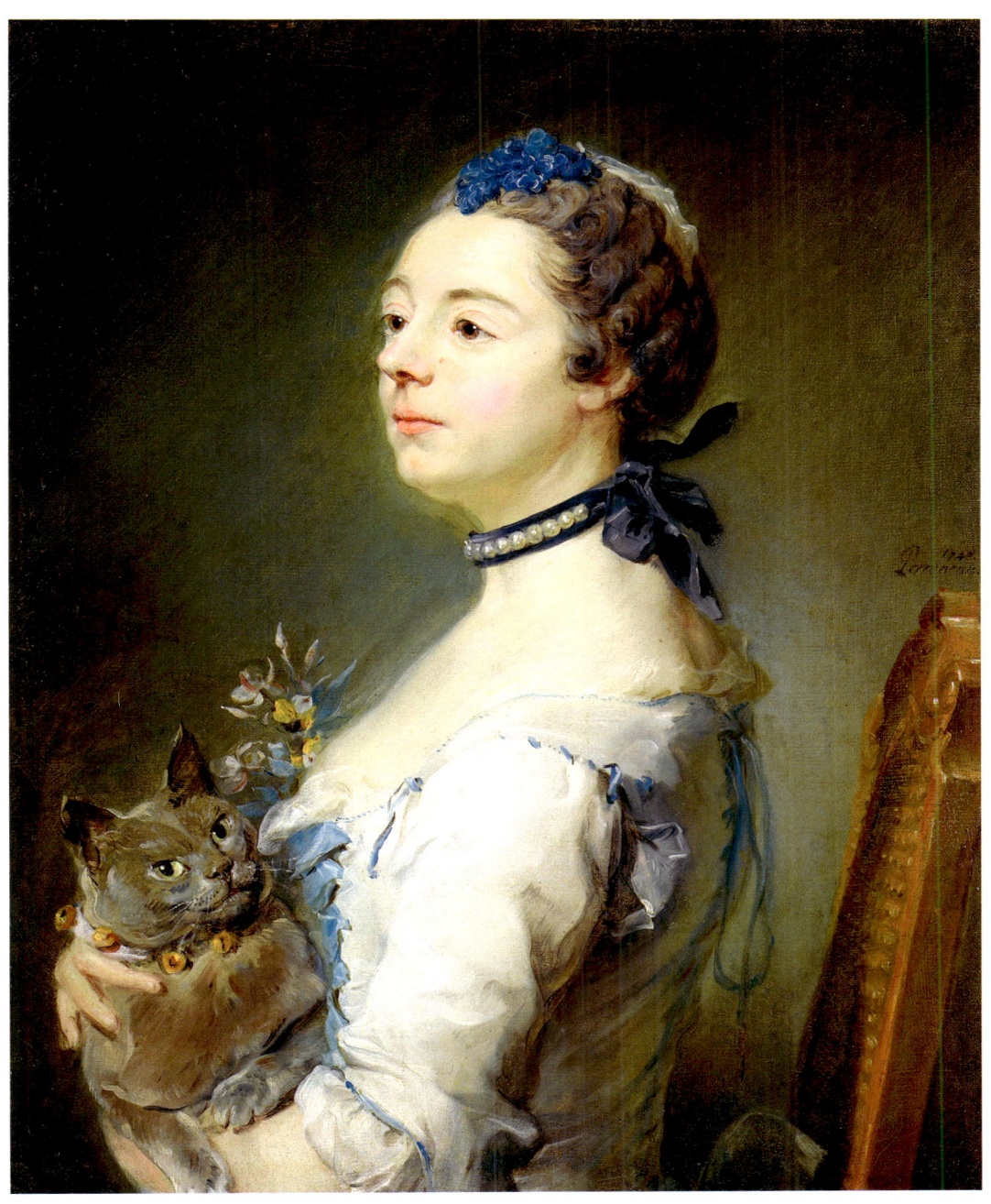

White Angora Cat Chasing a Butterfly

Around 1761

Exotic Elegance

The exotic cat arrives in Europe in the 18th century and becomes all the rage in aristocratic circles. Even the king has them at Versailles. The craze is such that it deserves to be represented alone on canvas.

Our white Angora is a luxurious, idle cat. Well-combed and, above all, well-fed by his masters, it no longer chases rodents around the house, but is content to gracefully follow butterflies in a garden. With its head turned, its paw in the air, and its tail in plume, the elegant feline sways against a backdrop of greenery. Supple, sinuous, and decorative as a Rocaille ornament.

The Angora cat is a much-appreciated novelty in the 18th century. Exotic cats—Persian, Syrian, and Angora—are imported from Iran, Syria, and Turkey. In the 17th and 18th centuries, the fascination with felines pours into Asia. Exoticism breathes new life into art and fashion. In his *Histoire Naturelle*, the naturalist Buffon devotes several historical and descriptive paragraphs to "Angora cats." The scientist praises their long, silky coat, round head, and variety of colors. Some Angoras are perfectly white, charming Westerners. While the dark, tabby European cat is still associated with deceit, savagery, and even misfortune and the Devil, these tabby cats enjoy great success.

Cardinal Richelieu, Louis XIII's chief minister, owns several cats, as does King Louis XV in the following century. We know the names of some of them: Blanchon and Brillant. Blanchon, as his name suggests, resembles the painting by Jean-Jacques Bachelier. He lives around 1730. Authorized to lounge on the fireplace in the king's cabinet, he also shares his bedroom, with a comfortable red damask cushion for a bed.

A Question of Style

Rocaille art flourishes between 1720 and 1770. Decorative, light, and refined, this typically French style is organized around **curved** lines and **asymmetry**. The Rocaille repertoire is inspired by the charms of **nature**: flowers, shells, birds, and clouds adorn aristocratic salons.

And the Dogs?

Small, fragile dogs are also in fashion. Pet **greyhounds** and small **spaniels** are all the rage at court. Louis XV loves his dogs to the point of dedicating portraits to them: Sylvie, Mignonne, Charlotte, and Gredinet are immortalized by the painter Oudry.

"There is nothing softer than the warm and vibrant hair of a cat, and nothing imparts to the skin a more delicate, refined, and rare sensation."

Guy de Maupassant

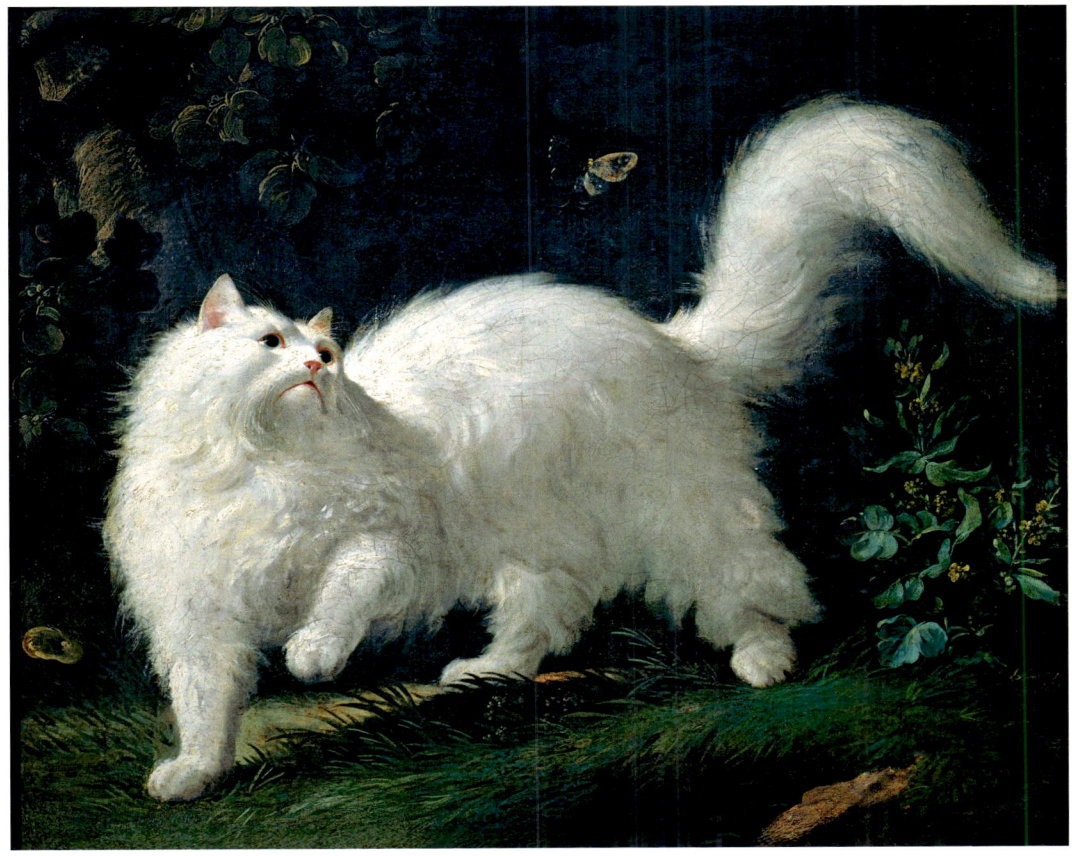

White Angora Cat Chasing a Butterfly
(Chat angora avec papillon)
Jean-Jacques Bachelier
Around 1761
Oil on canvas
Musée Lambinet, Versailles

Head of a Cat

1824

Feline Profiles

What is Romanticism?

This is a cultural and aesthetic movement of the early 19ᵗʰ century that seeks to break away from Greco-Roman references. **Literary subjects**, **exoticism**, **cathedrals**, or even the power of **nature** are the new themes favored by artists.

Eugène Delacroix, a Romantic painter par excellence, has a passion for depicting animals—tigers, lions, and horses populate his paintings. In his more intimate drawings and watercolors, the cat finds its place.

Delacroix did not produce any large-scale paintings featuring cats, but he often studied the feline in his sketches: quick drawings in black ink, graphite sketches, or watercolors on paper. His notebooks show cats playing, sleeping, stretching . . .

Our tabby cat head is his most accomplished study. It's detailed and colorful. The striped coat is precise. The ear is delicate and the whiskers fine. The little yellow eye is bright and the muzzle moist. The cat is depicted in profile, but its observant eye looks at us sideways. The cat is proud and upright, in the style of an Egyptian statue.

Watercolors are invented in England at the end of the 18ᵗʰ century, and the medium quickly becomes a success in Europe. It is widely used by Romantics. Easy and light to carry, it allows us to keep the spontaneity of the sketch by adding color. It's perfect for animal studies. Thanks to this technique, Delacroix gives his tigers, lions, and horses a striking illusion of life.

The artist's passion for felines is shared by other painters who, like him, are in search of the fiery and exotic. Théodore Géricault, for example, paints a majestic *Head of a Lion*. Tigers and lions are animals Delacroix studies while visiting the Ménagerie at the Jardin des Plantes in Paris.

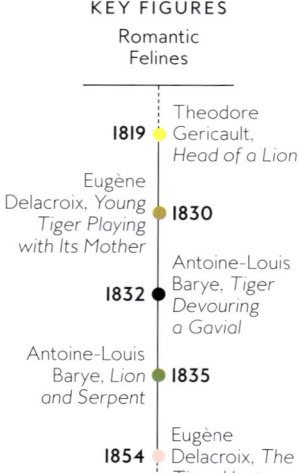

KEY FIGURES
Romantic Felines

1819 — Theodore Gericault, *Head of a Lion*

Eugène Delacroix, *Young Tiger Playing with Its Mother* — 1830

1832 — Antoine-Louis Barye, *Tiger Devouring a Gavial*

Antoine-Louis Barye, *Lion and Serpent* — 1835

1854 — Eugène Delacroix, *The Tiger Hunt*

Head of a Cat
(Tête de chat)
Eugène Delacroix
1824
Watercolor on paper
Musée du Louvre, Paris

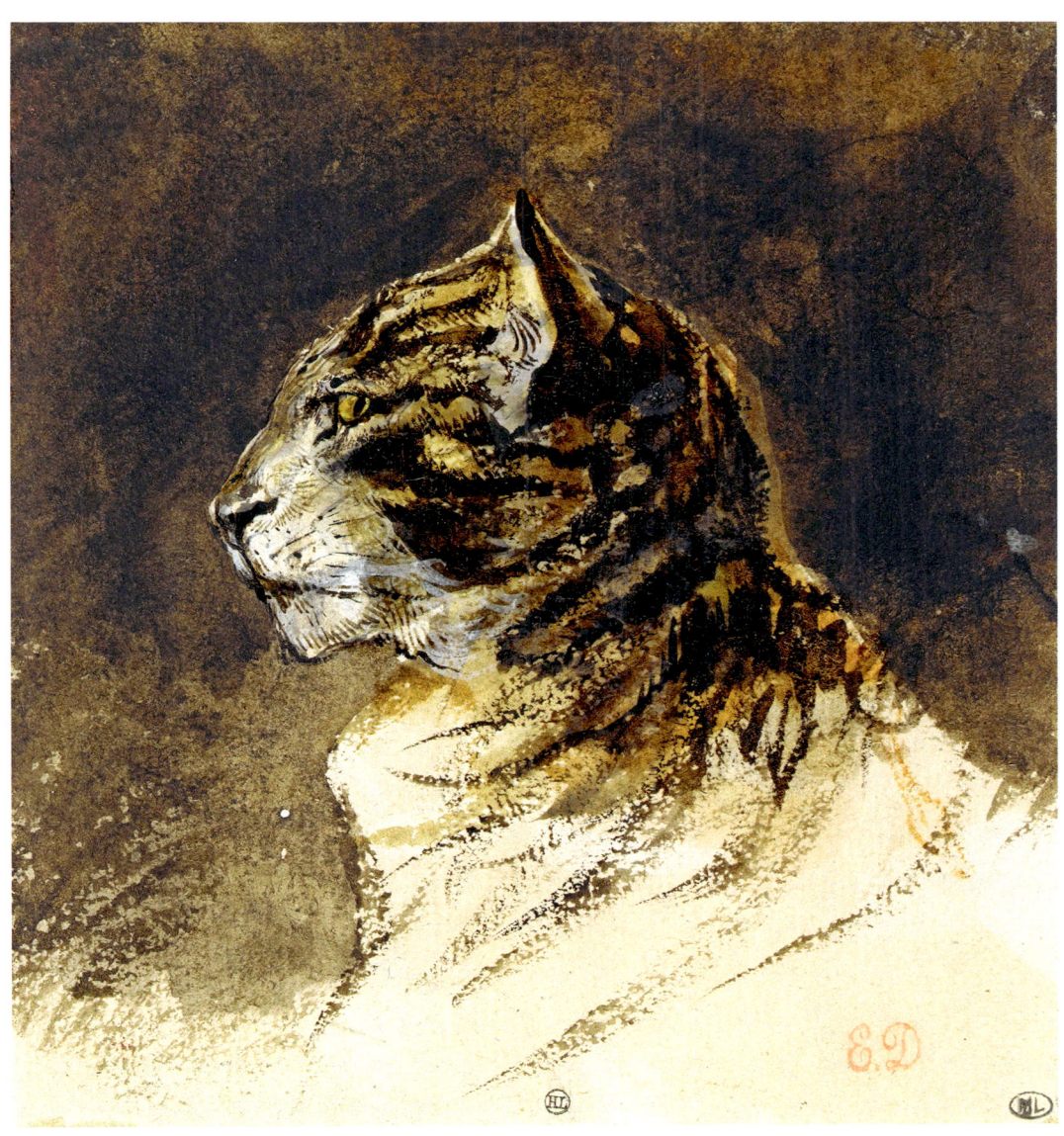

Olympia

1863

Prostitute, Maid, and Cat

Édouard Manet's *Olympia* is, without a doubt, one of the most important works of the 19th century. Somewhere between classical tradition and bold modernity, the painting features a prostitute, her maid, and her cat.

A woman lies on a bed with rumpled sheets. She stares straight into our eyes. Some call it a shameless stare. No doubt about it, she's a prostitute. Her maid, behind the bed, brings her a customer's bouquet. A spiky black cat rises to its feet. He looks at us, too, as if we've disturbed him by entering the room. Are we another customer?

Nothing is more scandalous in 1865 than this subject and its treatment: raw nudity, frank gaze, white skin with yellow accents. The painting is a laughingstock. Mockery, bad taste, and provocation are the order of the day. For the bourgeois, accustomed to pink mythological nudes, this woman is dirty, even cadaverous. Olympia is not a goddess with abstract nudity. She is an undressed woman. Worse still, she's dressed for work. Wearing her hair in a bun, she has kept her choker, earrings, and bracelet. She's half-shod.

This painting is best understood by looking at another: *Titian's Venus of Urbino* (1538). *Olympia* is a modernized version. At the foot of the Venus, a little dog sleeps. A symbol of fidelity, it echoes the theme of marriage. Manet replaces conjugal sexuality with paid sexuality. The goddess takes on flesh. The dog is replaced by a cat, an emblem of lasciviousness and sexuality. Black in color, it acquires an additional connotation in the 19th century, becoming the animal of urban nightlife.

"I did what I saw."

Édouard Manet

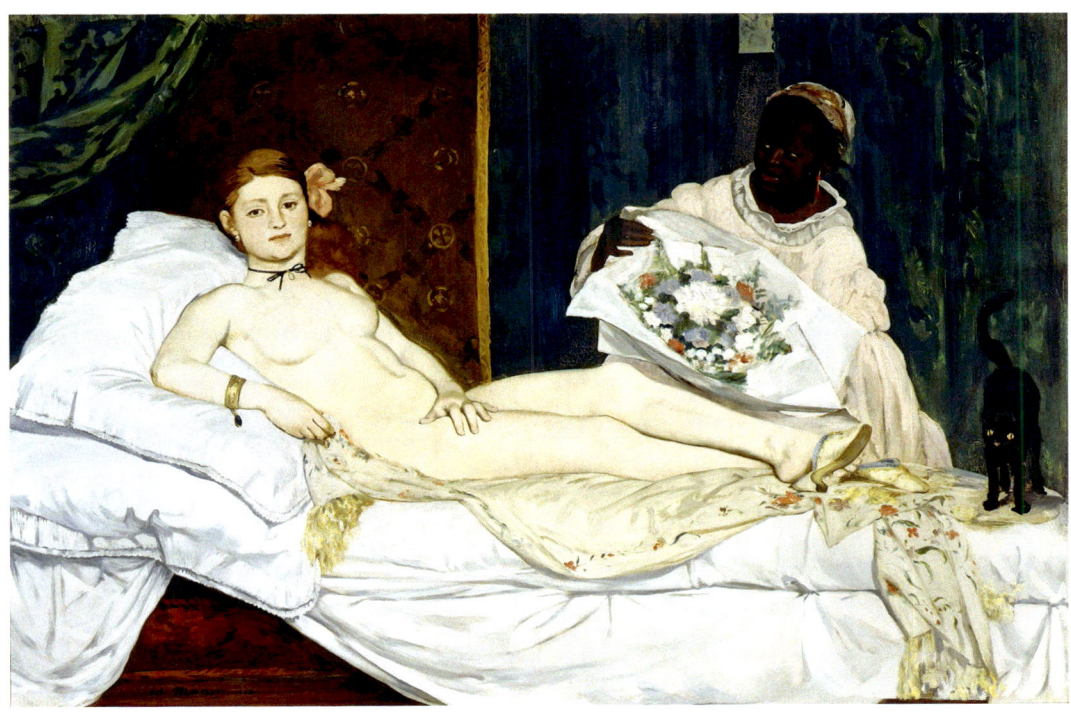

Olympia
Édouard Manet
1863
Oil on canvas
Musée d'Orsay, Paris

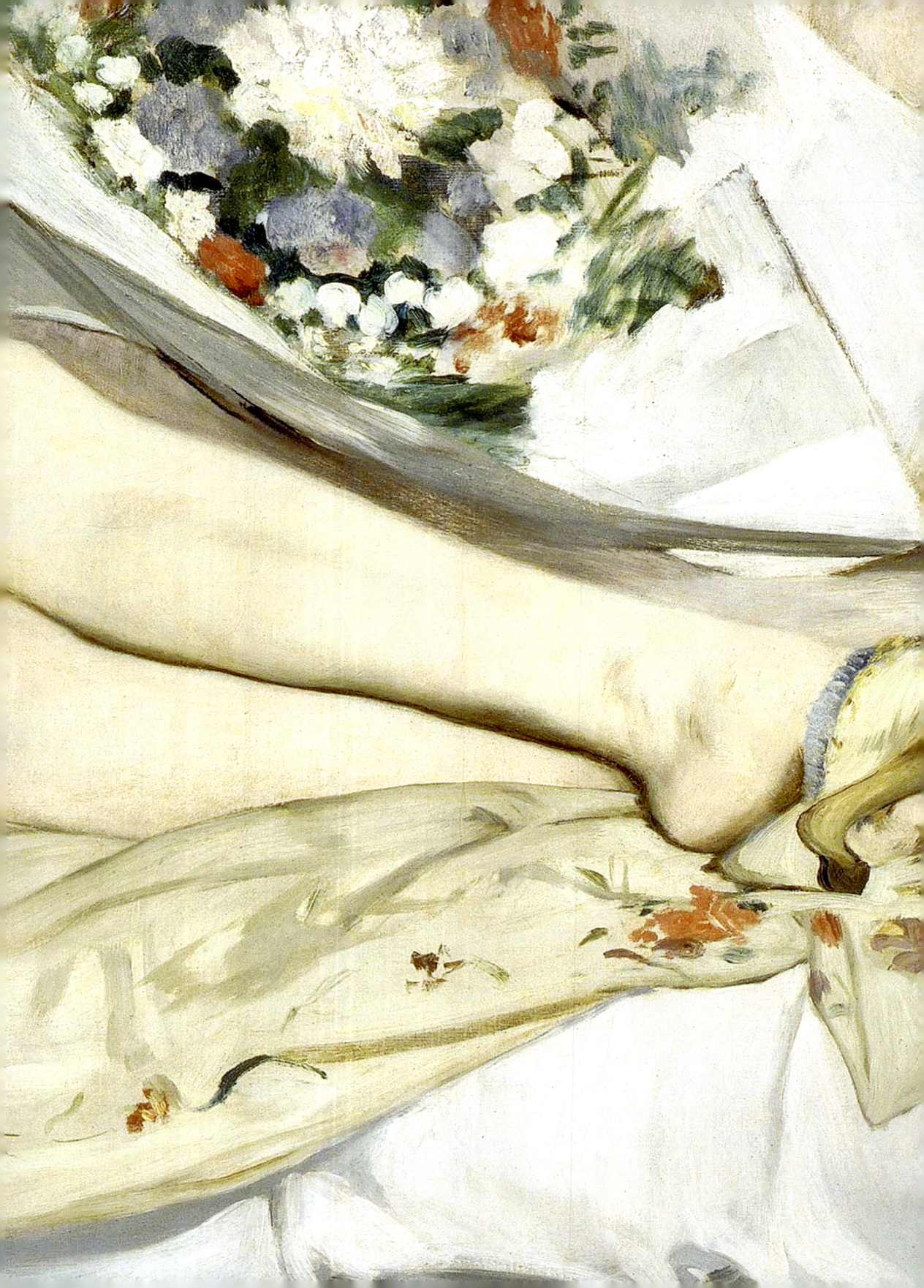

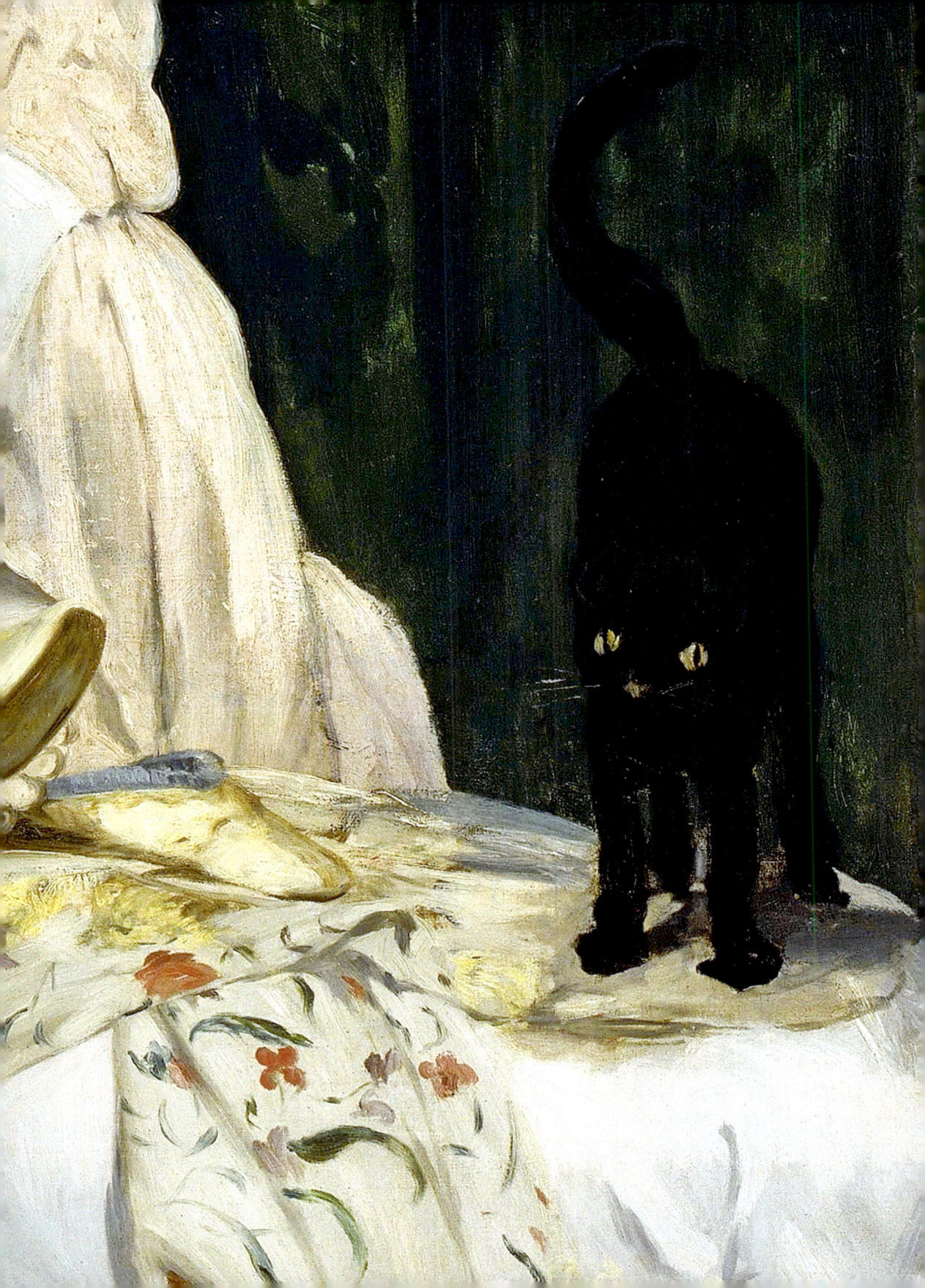

Puss in Boots

1862

KEY FIGURES
Names of
Cats

1200	Tibert (*Le Roman de Renart*)
Raminagrobis (*Fables*, Jean de La Fontaine)	**1668–1694**
1697	Puss in Boots (*Tales of My Mother Goose*, Charles Perrault)
Beau-Minon (*Blondine*, comtesse de Ségur)	**1856**
1865	The Cheshire Cat (*Alice in Wonderland*, Lewis Carroll)
Alphonse (*The Wonderful Farm, The Magic Pictures*, Marcel Aymé)	**1934–1946**

Puss in Boots
(*Le Chat botté appelant à l'aide*)
Gustave Doré
1862
Print
Bibliothèque nationale de France,
Paris

Once Upon a Time...

Every child knows Puss in Boots, the clever feline who stands and talks like a human. Hat, cape, and belt . . . he is one of a kind. But who knew that this outfit was created by Gustave Doré, the brilliant 19th-century illustrator?

"Help, help, my lord Marquis of Carabas is drowning!" shouts Puss in Boots, raising his paws. The feline stands on the bank while his master, a poor penniless miller's son, bathes naked in the river. It's only when he's noticed that the king in his carriage stops. The king hastens to offer the false marquis new clothes to replace his old ones, which he believes have been stolen by thieves, when, in fact, they have been hidden in a bush by the cunning tomcat.

A painter, but above all a virtuoso draughtsman, Gustave Doré illustrates the classics of literature. From 1855 to his death in 1883, nothing escapes him, from the Bible to Balzac, Dante, Rabelais, La Fontaine, Perrault, Chateaubriand, Edgar Allan Poe, or Victor Hugo. His Puss in Boots, Sleeping Beauty, and Little Red Riding Hood are still referenced today. Countless illustrators, cartoonists, and above all, filmmakers have drawn inspiration from his dreamlike world. He's a master of fantastic settings, teeming with detail, by turns magical or demonic.

"The Master Cat" or "Puss in Boots" is transcribed by Charles Perrault in his collection *Tales of My Mother Goose* in 1697. In the first illustrated version, the cat wears only a pair of boots. Doré dresses him in a Louis XIV period costume. The feline wears a broad-feathered hat, a noble cape, a leather purse, and a pair of extravagant boots. The artist adds some delightful feline details: the collar that closes the cape is made up of a row of small bird skulls, while in his purse a living mouse moves.

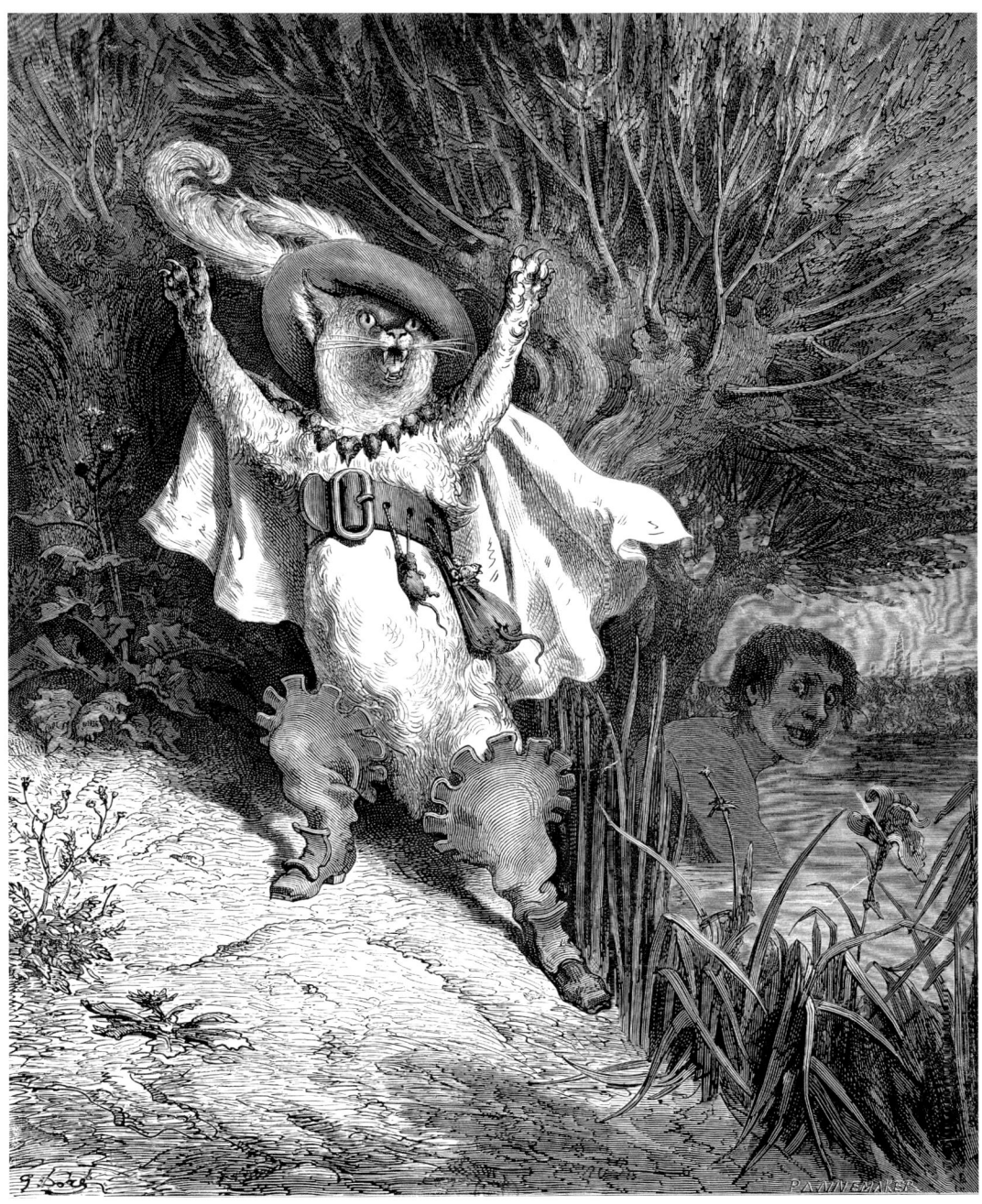

Young Boy with a Cat

1868

A Case Apart

Renoir and Cats

Renoir paints dozens of female portraits, from the **daughter** to the **mother** of the family. Many cats and kittens accompany the models, purring. Far from sexual undertones, they accentuate softness and comfort.

The Impressionists

1869: Monet and Renoir painted outdoors with a rapid brushstroke.
1874: First exhibition and birth of the word "Impressionism."
1876–1882: Organization of six exhibitions, without much success.
1886: Eighth and last exhibition, then separation from the group.
1900: Impressionists exhibit at the Universal Exhibition; beginning of their fame.

Young Boy with a Cat
(*Le Garçon au chat*)
Pierre Auguste Renoir
1868
Oil on canvas
Musée d'Orsay, Paris

Renoir is the Impressionist of women. Of his five thousand paintings, hundreds are studies of female nudes. At the beginning of his career, a unique and mysterious case appears: a naked young man with a cat.

A young boy with very white skin stands next to a piece of furniture covered with a long cloth. At his head, sitting on a green cushion, a large tomcat purrs. The cat rubs its head with delight on the cheek of the young man, who surrounds it with his arms. The presence of a cat next to a male nude is unprecedented. Here it creates an enigmatic sensual atmosphere.

In 1868, Pierre Auguste Renoir is at the very beginning of his career. He passes the entrance exam to the École des Beaux-Arts in Paris six years earlier, where he meets three young painters his own age: Claude Monet, Frédéric Bazille, and Alfred Sisley. Impressionism does not yet exist; the movement was officially born in 1874. In the late 1860s, Renoir was still searching for his style. He works from a live model and looks at the works of Courbet and Manet. The raw and daring realism of their nudes fascinates him. Manet's *Olympia* (see page 31), unveiled to the public just three years before he painted *Young Boy with a Cat*, has a profound impact on him: the very pale skin of the model contrasting with the dark background, the bottle-green cushion identical to the curtain in *Olympia*, and even the cat.

Young Boy with a Cat is without equal in Renoir's work. It is his only male nude. No one knows the model's identity. Is it a simple studio model? The painter never returned to this theme. He is too passionate about women and jokes about it himself: "I didn't know how to walk yet, but I already loved women!"

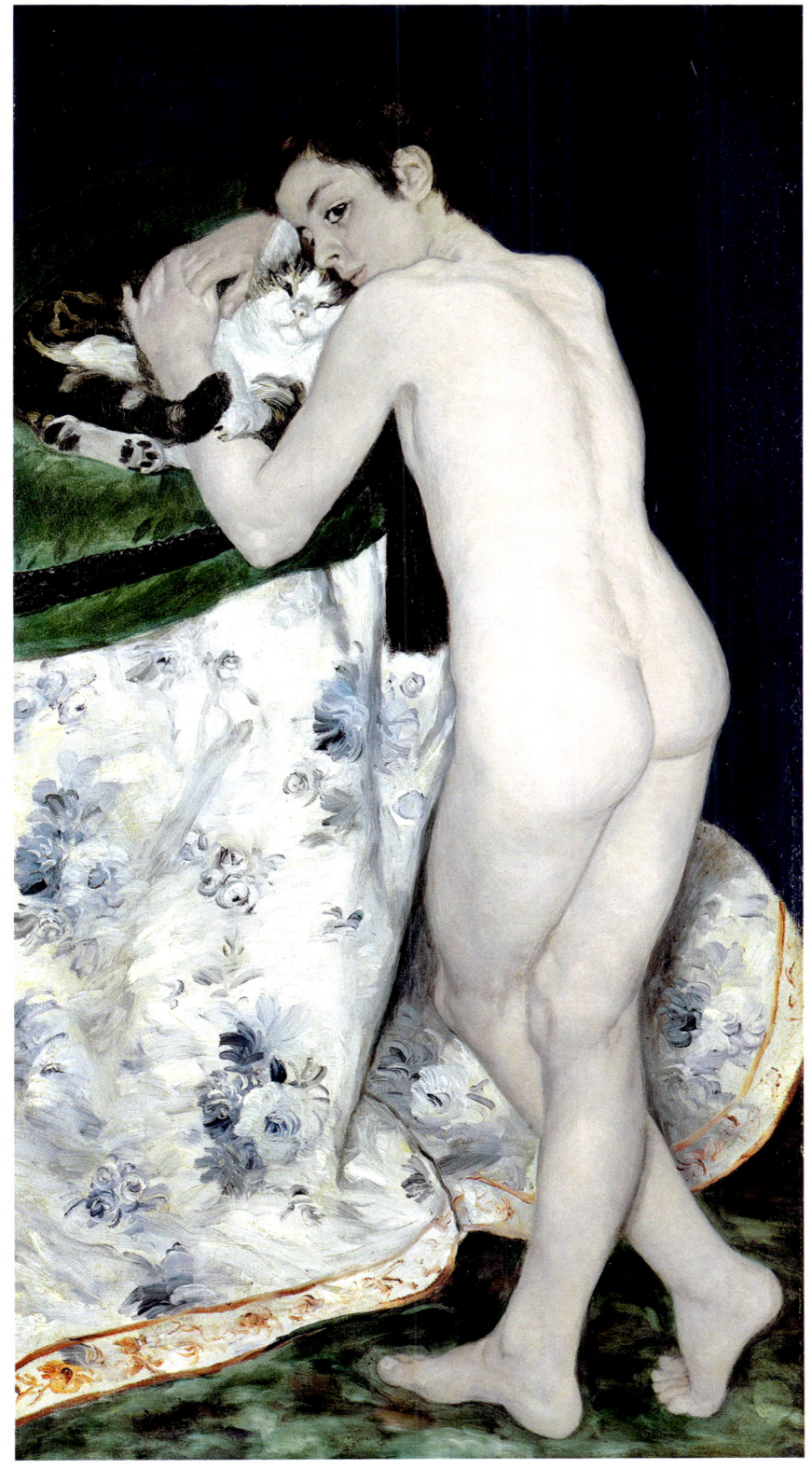

The White Cat

1894

Gentle Awakening

A painter of the poetry of small things, Bonnard depicts animals with great tenderness. This long-legged white cat, strange and comical, is the most famous of his felines.

A white cat stretches out after a nap. It stiffens his paws, buries its head in its neck and squints contentedly. It wrinkles its pink muzzle while its mouth almost breaks into a smile. Bonnard paints his cat waking up in the garden with kindness and amusement. The cat has just emerged from a moment of gentle torpor. We can imagine it napping in its favorite corner of the garden on a pleasant summer afternoon.

The light is soft and the cat casts no shadow. The absence of shadow is common with Pierre Bonnard. He will work throughout his career to render light and its quivering. And then there's the Japanese influence, the famous "pictures of the floating world." Like his Nabis friends—Maurice Denis, Félix Vallotton, Paul Ranson, Édouard Vuillard—he collects Japanese art. Prints, screens, and kakemonos were an infinite source of inspiration. His love of Japanese art, in which the cat is abundantly represented, earns him the nickname "Japanese Nabi" from his friends.

Bonnard likes to populate his works with animals that are dear to him. Thus, we meet his cats, his dogs, the chickens from the family farm in Isère . . . He works with a touch inherited from Impressionism, playing with color scales. This mottled hue is unique. It sets him apart from the other Nabis, who often favored flat tints (see pages 91 and 95). Bonnard thus wonderfully captures the softness of the white cat's fur and, above all, the pleasant shiver that runs through its entire body, from the bottom of the legs to the tip of the tail.

(see pages 91 and 95)

Bonnard Said

Bonnard loves **nature**, **light**, and the **outdoors**. Once while visiting the Musée du Louvre in Paris, he exclaims: "The most beautiful things in a museum are the windows."

Not So Simple . . .

Bonnard hesitates for a long time about the shape and **position** of *The White Cat's* **legs**. In addition to several preparatory drawings, an **X-ray** analysis of the painting reveals numerous alterations. Some are even visible to the naked eye.

The White Cat
(*Le Chat blanc*)
Pierre Bonnard
1894
Oil on cardboard
Musée d'Orsay, Paris

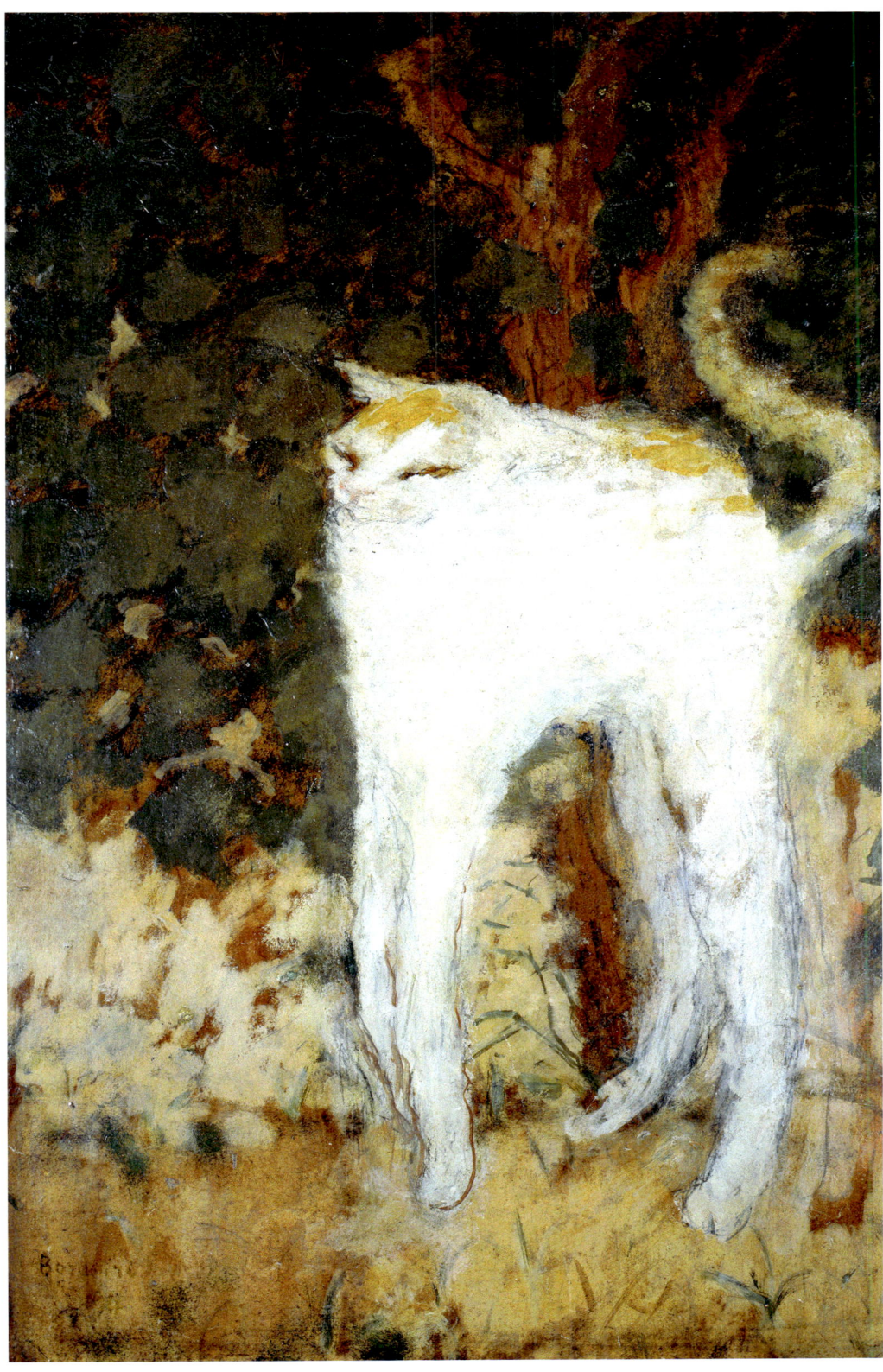

Tour of Rodolphe Salis' Chat Noir

1896

La Ballade du Chat Noir

The singer **Aristide Bruant** is a friend of **Toulouse-Lautrec**, who signs his posters. The composer and performer of *La Ballade du Chat Noir* is considered the creator of the chanson réaliste. His style lasted until **Édith Piaf**.

Cabarets of the Belle Époque

Folies-Bergère: founded in 1869
Le Chat Noir: 1881–1897
Le Moulin Rouge: founded in 1889
La Belle Meunière: for the 1900 Universal Exhibition

Tour of Rodolphe Salis' Chat Noir
(Tournée du Chat Noir de Rodolphe Salis)
Théophile Alexandre Steinlen
1896
Lithograph
LACMA, Los Angeles

Mysterious Icon

Steinlen's black cat is as much a figure of Paris as the silhouette of the Eiffel Tower. Before invading souvenir stores, it was the emblem of a famous Belle Époque cabaret.

Painter and sculptor Théophile Alexandre Steinlen leaves his native Switzerland for Paris in 1881. A libertarian and anarchist, he loves working-class Paris. He settles in Montmartre and meets the artistic personalities who gravitated there. He meets Rodolphe Salis, who opens his cabaret Le Chat Noir at the foot of the hill the same year. The place quickly becomes a popular meeting place for all of Paris. Tourists, bankers, doctors, prostitutes, journalists, and artists are all to be found here. Among the regulars are Toulouse-Lautrec, Alphonse Allais, and Aristide Bruant.

Familiar with the area, Steinlen is also a lover cats. The one he draws for the poster is seated, proud and slender. A graphic cat, halfway between Art Nouveau and the ancient Egypt that fascinates him. The lines are curved, the graphics simple, and the layout effective. Steinlen is also a satirical press illustrator, drawing for the famous weekly *L'Assiette au beurre*. Its free style borders on caricature: the black cat's whiskers are fanciful and immense, its coat shaggy, its paws clawed. His cat is treated as a solid black silhouette, a black silhouette of which only the piercing eyes are visible. The cabaret also offers a shadow theater.

Rehabilitated by the Romantics in the mid-19th century, the alley cat, or black cat, finally finds its letters of nobility. It is associated with Parisian bohemian life in the 1900s. The ideal companion of penniless artists and solitary writers, it is like its masters: both integrated and on the fringes of society, urban, a night owl, and above all . . . mysterious.

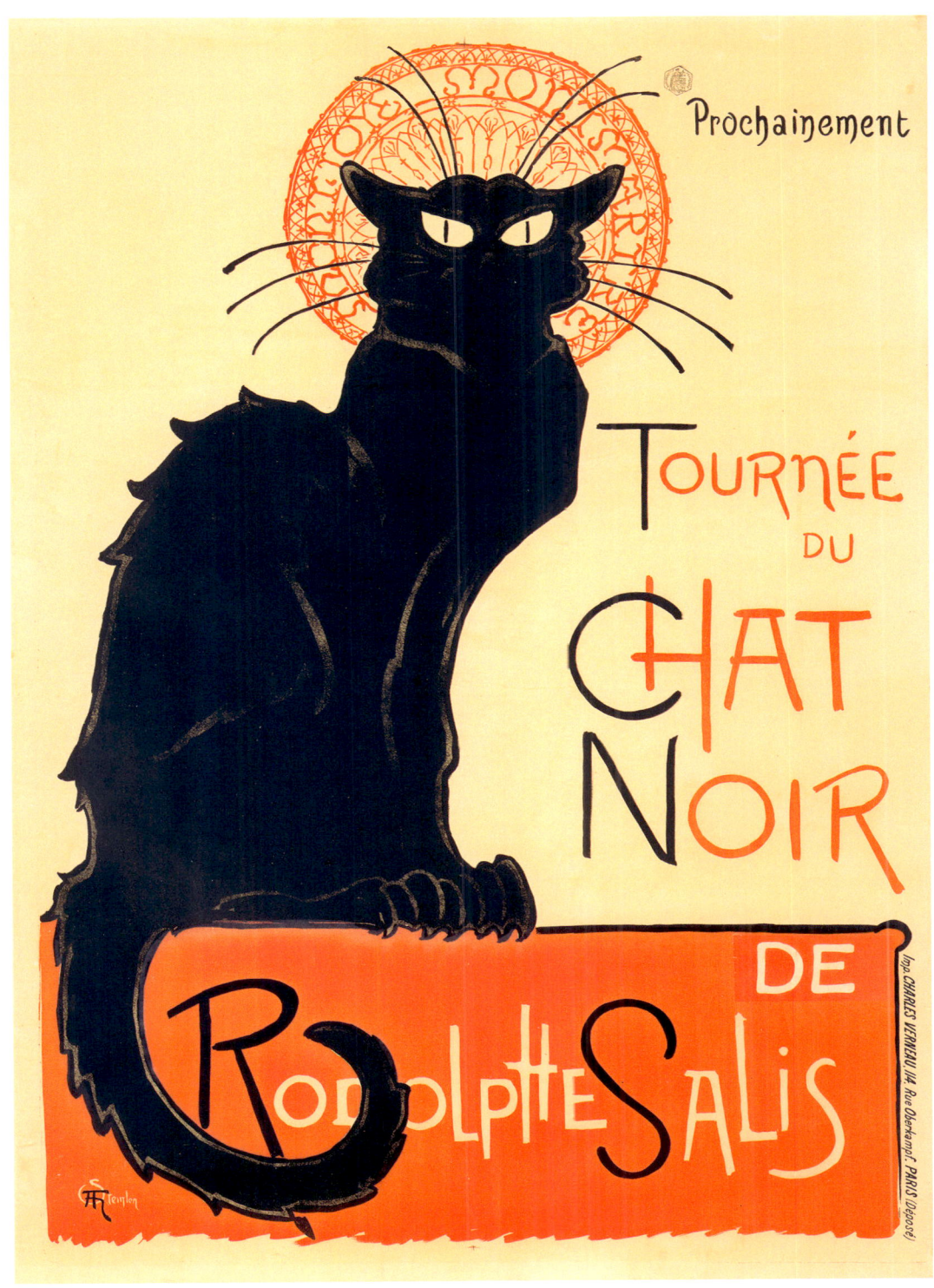

The Artist's Mother

1904

Purring Away

Often referred to as a "late Impressionist" or "softened Fauve," Marquet is one of Matisse's best friends. A discreet, poetic painter, he loves fluid landscapes, subtle colors, and quiet portraits.

In this pastel drawing, he depicts his mother. She is immersed in her embroidery work. On her lap, a big gray cat purrs peacefully. The cat has closed its eyes and rests its head on the white tips of its paws. It looks as comfortable as possible. Its lowered head echoes the face of its mistress, whose meticulous activity happily guarantees him a long nap. A lively yet subtle range of reds, browns, and grays gives this interior scene a reassuring atmosphere.

Marquet is very close to his mother and often paints her. He enjoys these simple moments with her. Born in Bordeaux, the artist comes from a modest background. An only child, he has a difficult childhood: he is nearsighted, frail, and afflicted with a club foot. The young man soon finds refuge in drawing, filling his school notebooks with sketches. His mother, Marguerite Deyres, is a devoted woman. She supports her son and wants him to be able to study drawing and painting in Paris. Against the advice of his father, a railroad employee who has little faith in Albert's talent, the mother and the teenager pack their bags. They both settle in Paris in 1890, on rue Monge. His mother opens a boutique and her son enters the École des Arts Décoratifs. There he meets Henri Matisse, with whom he forges a lasting friendship.

Nothing in this tranquil image, except perhaps the bright red of the dress, suggests that Marquet is rubbing shoulders with the most avant-garde painters. He exhibits alongside the Fauves Matisse, Vlaminck, and Derain at the 1905 Salon d'Automne.

The Artist's Mother
(Portrait de la mère de l'artiste)
Albert Marquet
1904
Pastel on paper
Musée des Beaux-Arts, Bordeaux

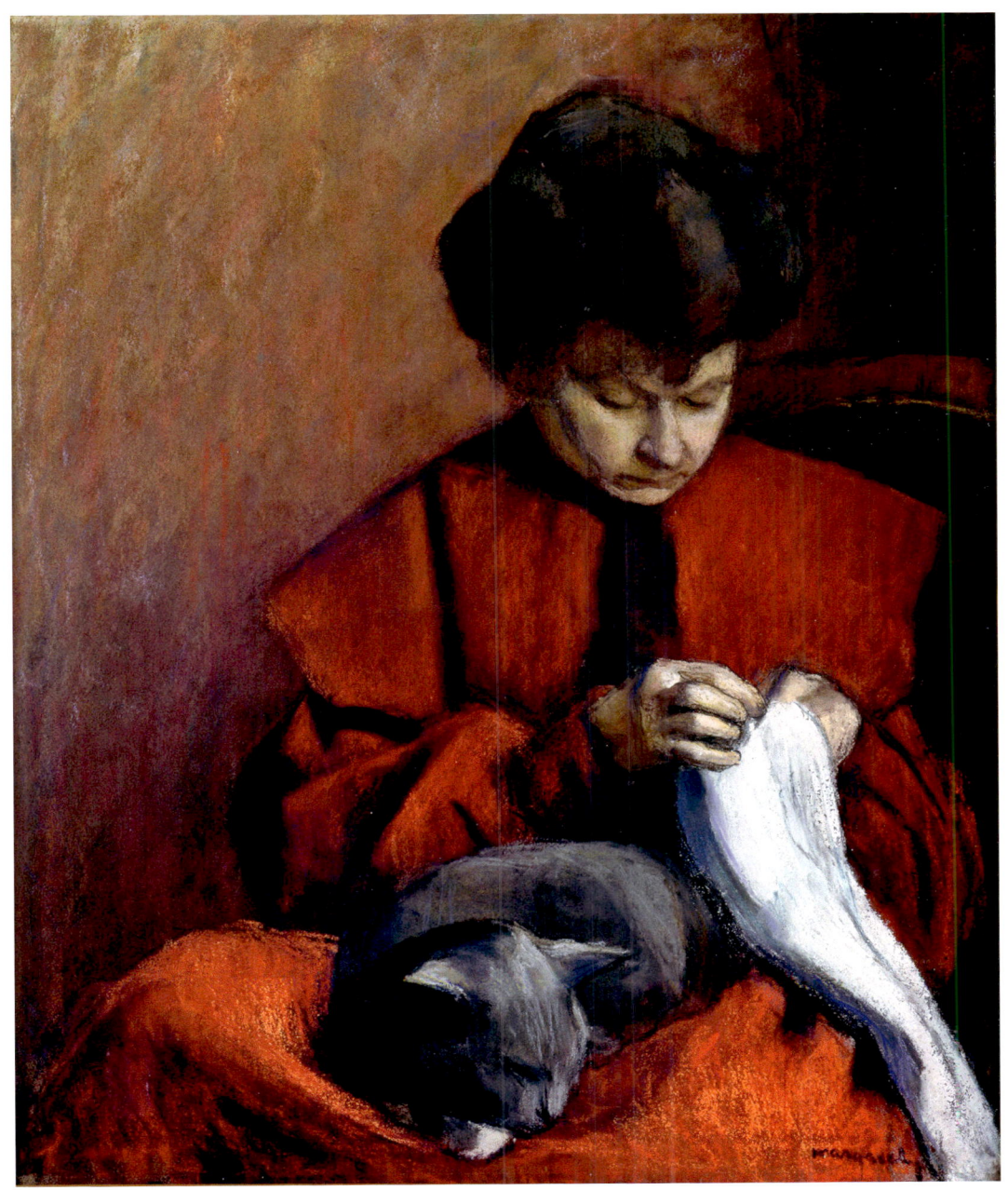

Girl with a Black Cat

1910

Harmony

1910

This is an important year for Matisse. In addition to a series of female portraits, he completes the creation, for the Russian collector **Shchukin**, of two of his greatest masterpieces: *The Dance* and *Music*.

Henri Matisse often lived with cats. Yet they never appear in his paintings. Never, except once: on his daughter's lap.

In 1910, Marguerite is sixteen years old. From a fragile child, she becomes a blossoming teenager. This portrait strikes a delicate balance between stylization and likeness. The cat is Marguerite's favorite. Its big, black-rimmed eyes look at us with modesty. They respond to the deep black of her hair and that of the cat's own body. After the brief and dazzling period of Fauvism, during which Matisse abandons black, he once again explores its possibilities. The supple and powerful contour line becomes one of his signatures.

Marguerite's black cat is above all a motif, just like her hair. Their curved forms respond perfectly to each other. The cat is treated as a flat surface, without any detail, like a Chinese shadow or a paper cutout before its time. Between the black shapes, the colors vibrate. The white and blue of the outfit are framed by the yellow of the armchair. The touch of color is always visible, sometimes streaked, sometimes brushed. The abstract background is green and pink. A touch of green on Marguerite's forehead and her rosy cheeks echo this. With Matisse, it's always a question of balance and harmony.

Marguerite is the eldest child, born to Matisse and his first wife. His second wife, Amélie, considers her his daughter. At the age of six, Marguerite suffers from severe diphtheria. In poor health, she is unable to attend school normally. She's always stuffed in the workshop and becomes a favored model. As an adult, she marries and disappears from the canvas. But she remains close to her father: she acts as his secretary, represents him at exhibitions, and works on establishing his catalog raisonné.

Girl with a Black Cat
(Marguerite au chat noir)
Henri Matisse
1910
Oil on canvas
Musée National d'Art Moderne, Centre Pompidou, Paris

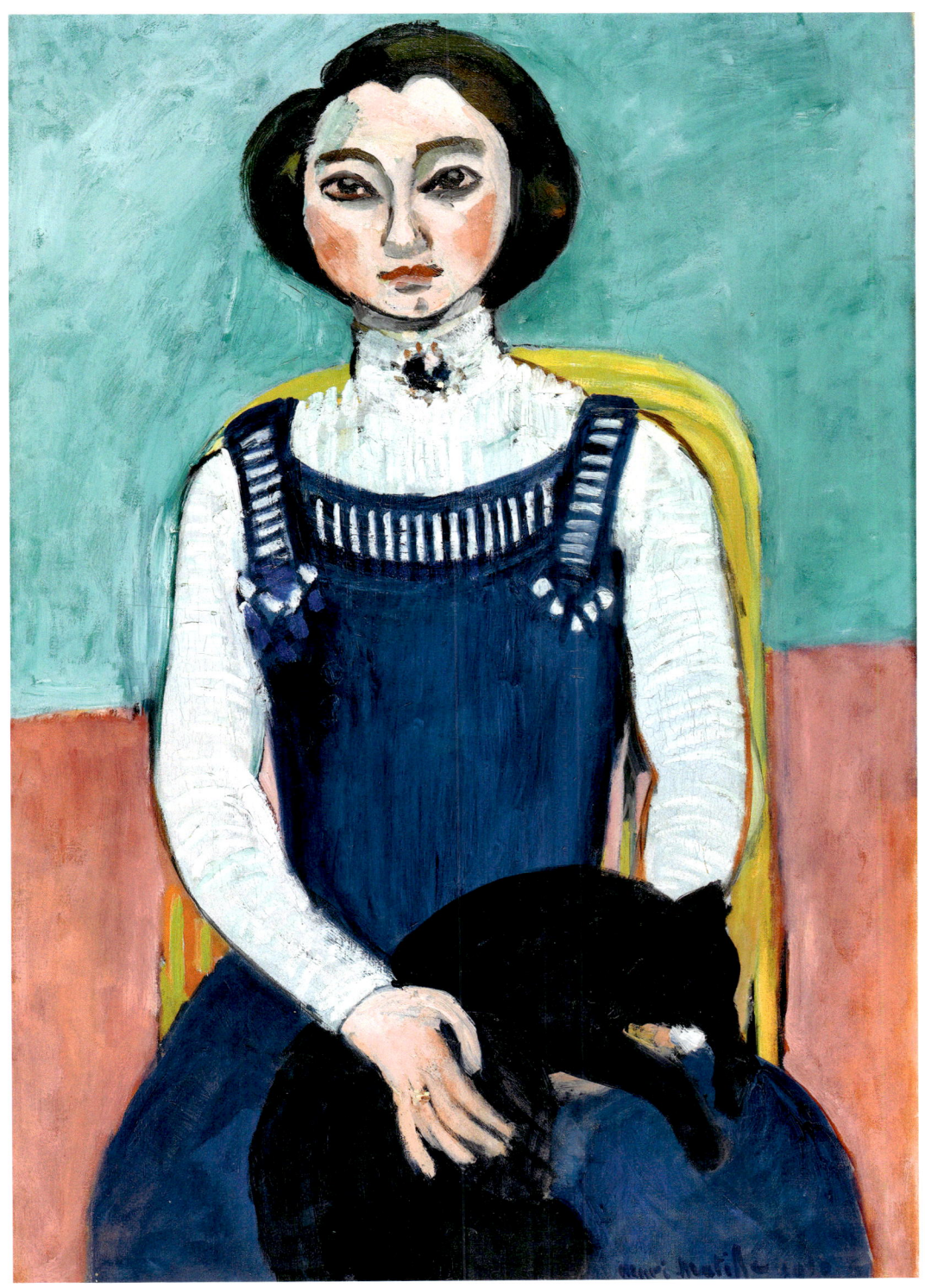

Three Cats

1913

A Friend to Animals

A Few Dates

1905: Birth of Fauvism (France)
1905: Formation of Die Brücke Expressionist group (Germany)
1907: Birth of Cubism (France)
1909: Birth of Rayonism (Russia)
1909: Publication of the *Futurist Manifesto* (Italy)
1912: Formation of Der Blaue Reiter Expressionist group (Germany)
1914: First World War begins, end of avant-garde movements

Franz Marc has always preferred the purity of animals to the society of men, which is too far removed from nature. Dogs, horses, cows, deer, wolves, and cats are all part of his brief and intense career.

Franz Marc has painted three wildcats, large blades of grass, and a tree trunk. Despite these few recognizable elements, the work is halfway between figuration and abstraction. Right in the middle, one cat stretches out in a dynamic, powerful movement. The other two are seated. One, huge and red, sits behind the black-and-white cat, though much larger. The red cat observes us, lowering its head as if to enter the frame. On the right, a tabby cat turns its head towards us.

Marc is part of the German Expressionist painters Der Blaue Reiter (The Blue Rider). Fascinated, like his friends Vassily Kandinsky and August Macke, by the expressive power of line and color, the artist moves away from reality to embrace abstract art. The bodies of the cats are simplified and treated in facets, like early cubist works by Braque and Picasso. The colors are reminiscent of Matisse's Fauvism. As for the dynamic stretching of the central cat, it continues the explorations of Italian Futurist artists. His painting also follows in the footsteps of the Russian Rayonists, who seek to capture the energy of matter through rays.

Breaking away from the modern industrial world, Franz Marc finds his favorite theme in animals. He sees man as a corrupt being but celebrates the purity of animals, in symbiosis with nature. At the beginning of his career, he paints round and benevolent animals: horses, cows, and dogs. In 1913, with the approach of war, concern began to make itself felt. With broken lines, he depicts wilder animals: wolves, a tiger, and our three cats.

"I found people ugly very early on; animals seemed to me more beautiful, more pure."
Franz Marc

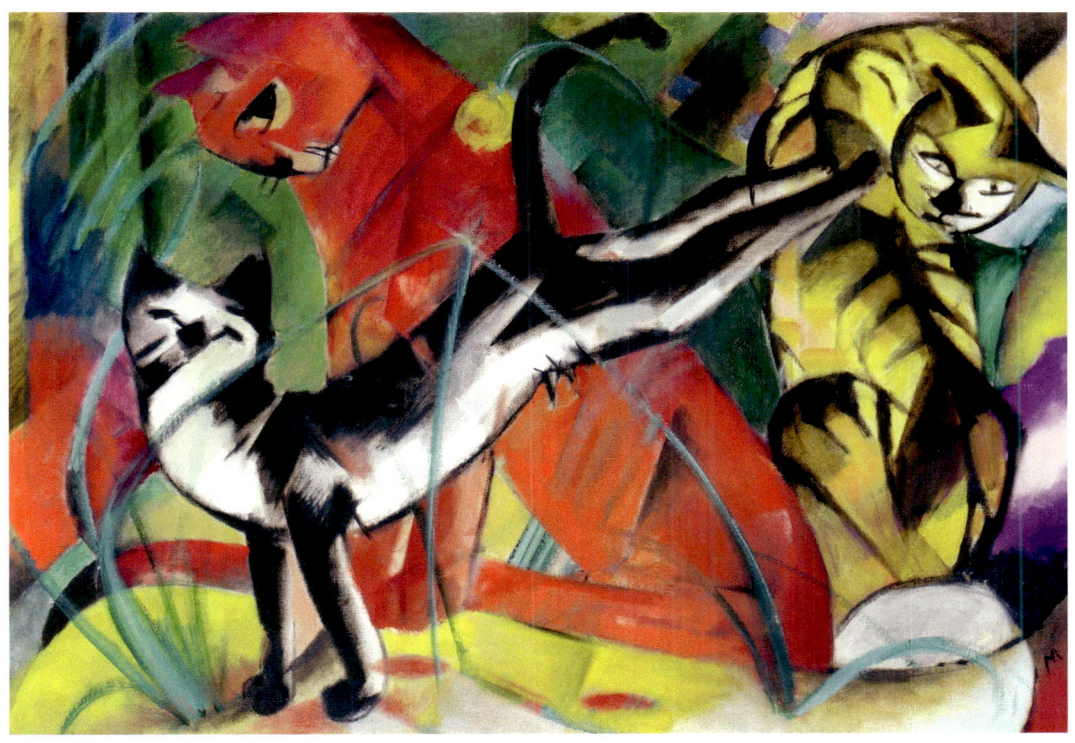

Three Cats
(Drei Katzen)
Franz Marc
1913
Oil on canvas
Kunstsammlung Nordrhein–
Westfalen, Düsseldorf

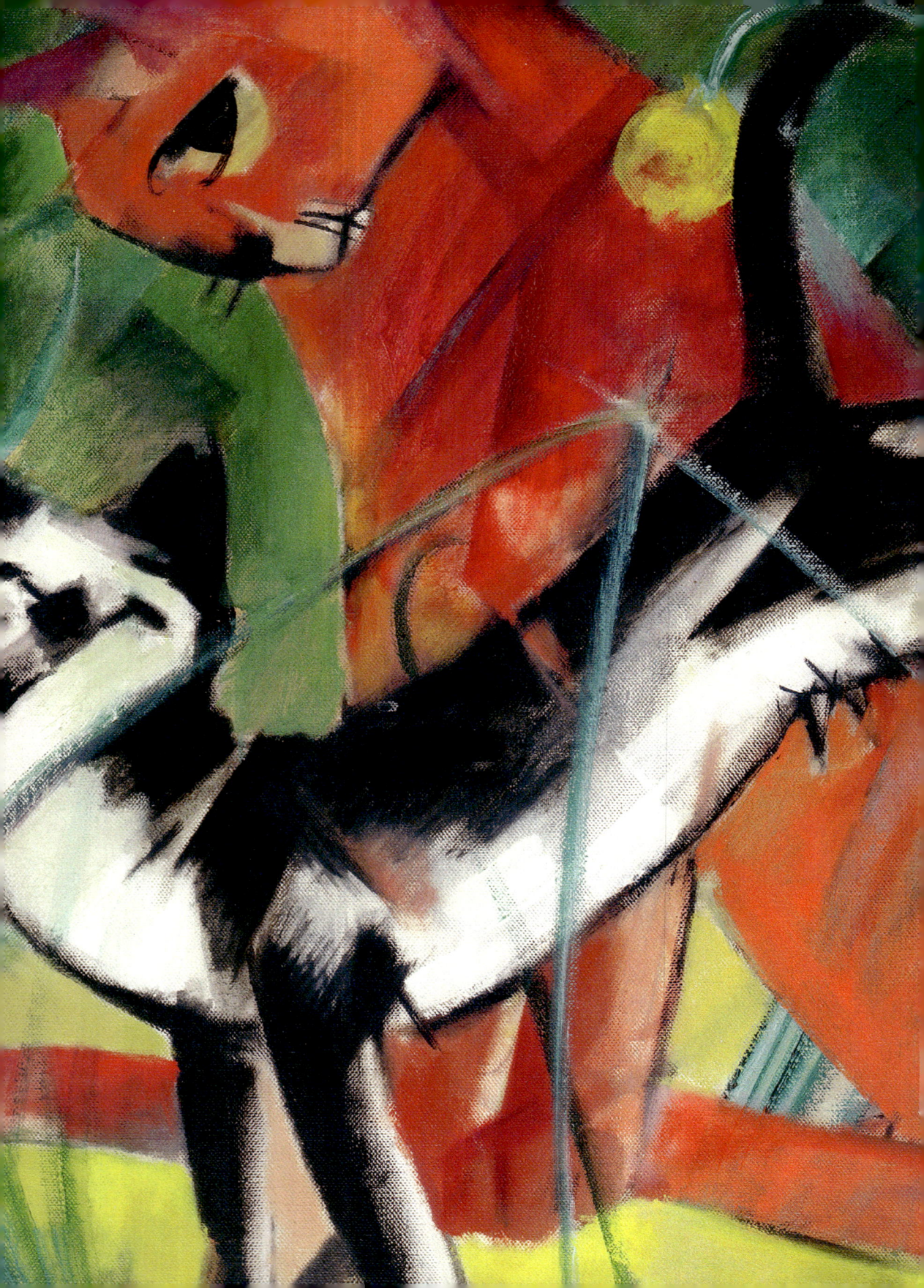

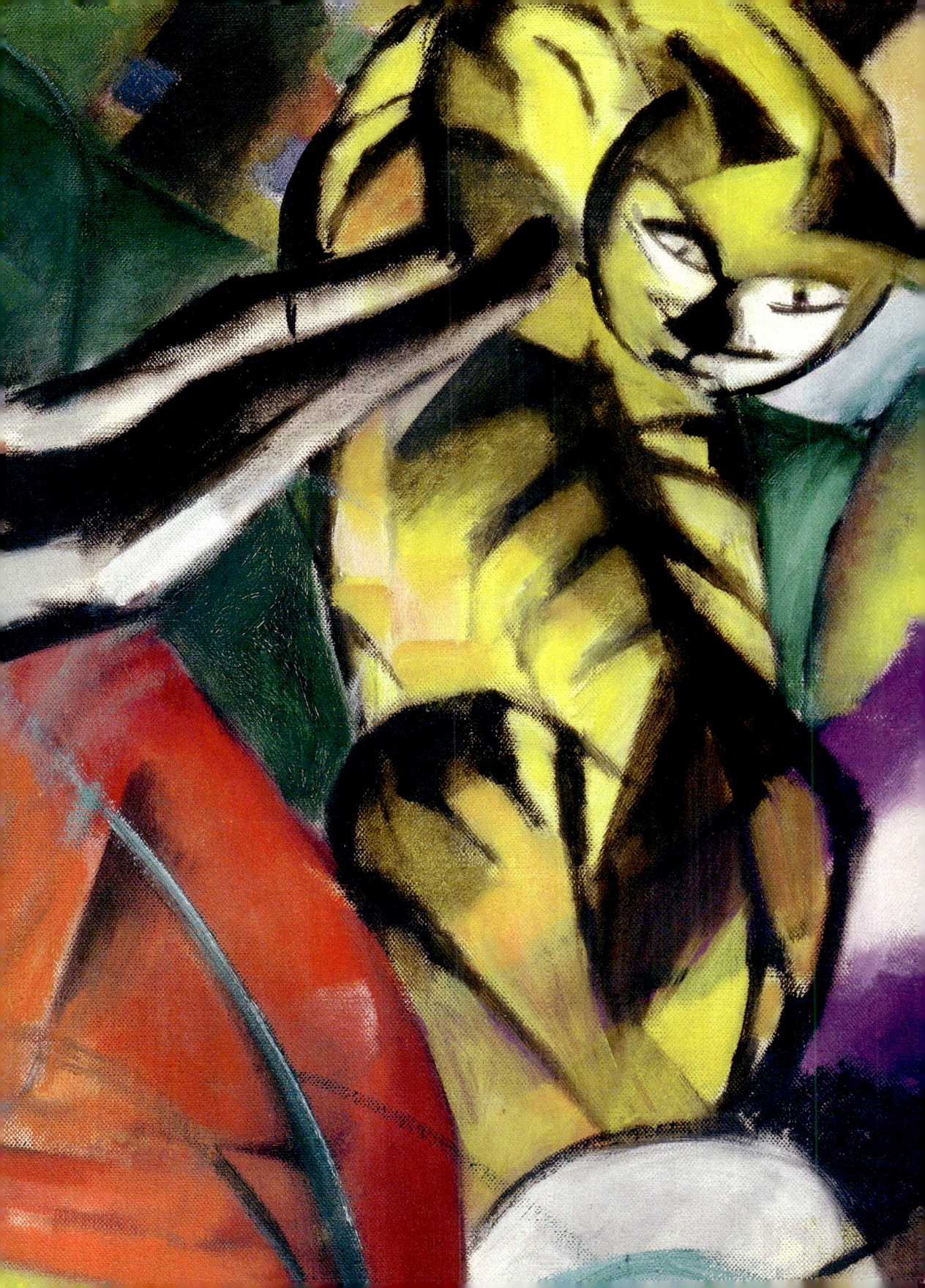

White Cat

France–Japan

Felines populate the world of Foujita, nicknamed the "Painter of Cats." A voluptuous companion in female nudes with milky bodies and an admirer of the painter in Foujita's self-portraits, the cat is the benevolent and silent friend.

A white cat stares at us with its almond-shaped eyes. To be honest, this cat is not perfectly white, it is tricolored. Its coat is spotted with beige and black. The black spots are elegant commas that adorn the feline's forehead, round back, and tip of the tail. Echoing these two colors, the gray of the floor and the pale pink of the wall are the only hues in the background.

Foujita likes to depict everyday life with meticulous detail. The whiskers, the hair of the tail or the ear, are of rare finesse. These delicate strokes are reminiscent of traditional Japanese ink paintings. Similarly, the sparse use of color evokes the purity of Asian art.

Foujita's art, so popular in the 1920s, is a skillful mix of East and West. Born in Japan, he studies at the Tokyo School of Fine Arts before moving to Paris in 1913. The cat is a very popular animal and is abundantly represented in Japanese culture. It appears in the prints of the 19th century masters Hiroshige, Hokusai, and Kuniyoshi. At the same time, in France during the Roaring Twenties, cats become the companions of artists and intellectuals. Our feline is, therefore, a condensed version of the artist's dual culture.

The elegance of cats is matched by that of Foujita. Bowl cut, earrings, fine mustache, and homemade clothes: the Japanese dandy is a fixture at Montparnasse society parties.

Evil or Lucky?

Introduced to Japan in medieval times, the cat is a dual animal. The **Bakeneko**, or **cat monster**, is a cat with evil supernatural powers. The famous **Manekineko**, on the other hand, is the tricolor **lucky cat** that raises its paw and calls for good fortune.

Miké the Friend

In the 1920s–1930s, **Foujita** lives with his cat **Miké**, a faithful companion who never lets him out of its sight. Miké is not white, it is tabby brown. In Foujita's self-portraits, it always looks lovingly at its master.

"The ideal of calm exists in a sitting cat."

Jules Renard

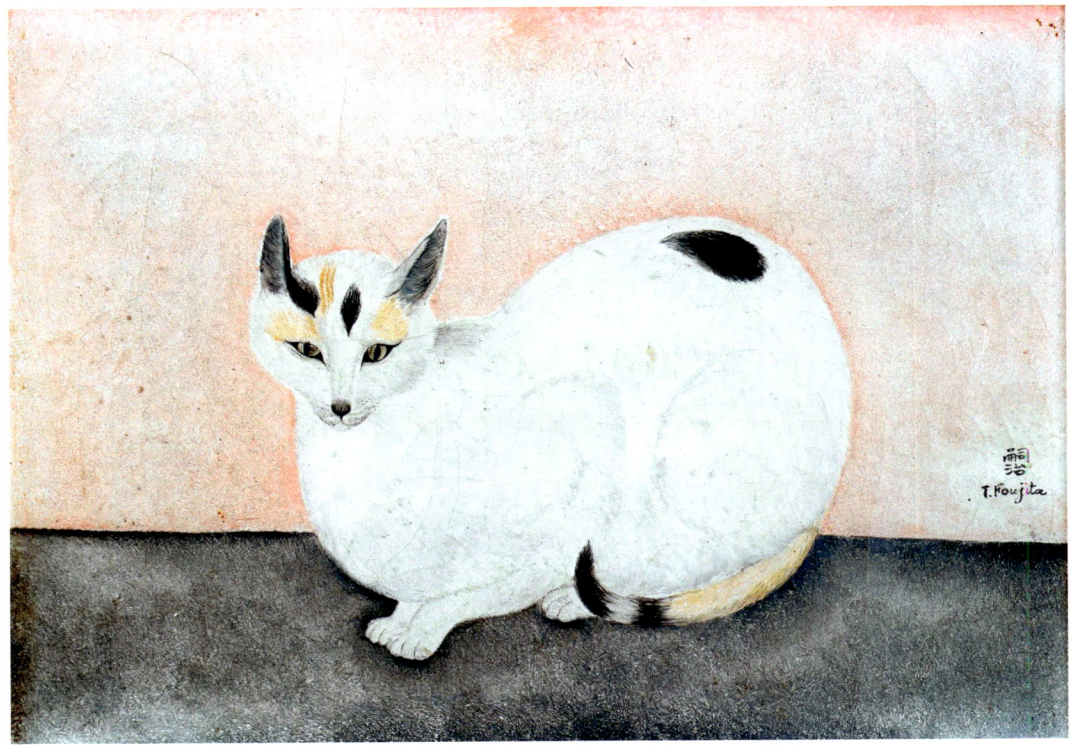

White Cat
(Le Chat blanc)
Léonard Tsuguharu Foujita
1920
Oil on canvas
Private collection

The King of Cats

1935

I Am a Cat

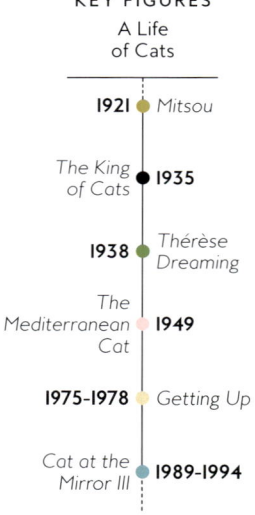

KEY FIGURES
A Life
of Cats

1921 · *Mitsou*

The King of Cats ● 1935

1938 ● *Thérèse Dreaming*

The Mediterranean Cat ● 1949

1975–1978 ● *Getting Up*

Cat at the Mirror III ● 1989–1994

The King of Cats
(*Le Roi des chats*)
Balthus
1935
Oil on canvas
Fondation Beyeler, Riehen

Balthus is an artist apart. He is not part of any movement. The cat, recurrent in his work, is his totem animal, not to say his alter ego.

The twenty-seven-year-old young man plays with his lanky physiognomy, stretching his legs out excessively. A big tabby cat rubs its head against his right knee. To his left, a plaque is leaning against a stool, on which rests a whip. The inscription reads: "The portrait of H. M. the King of Cats painted by Himself, MCMXXXV." We are therefore faced with the "portrait of His Majesty the king of cats painted by himself." This king baffles us . . . ironic or megalomaniac?

As usual, Balthus deploys an ambivalent universe. We oscillate between the gentleness of the cat and the violence of the whip. We hesitate between the dandy's relaxed attitude, with his hand on his hip, and the dark gaze with which he stares at us. The artist is going through a complicated period. His erotic and ambiguous works, exhibited the previous year in Paris, caused a scandal. He has sold almost nothing and feels so misunderstood that he considers ending his life. He now lives with a cat, the one in the portrait, whom he has named Frightener. A cat who scares everyone except his master.

Behind the representation of Frightener is certainly the memory of Mitsou, the cat to whom Balthus owes his early entry onto the artistic scene. At the age of eleven, he adopts and then loses Mitsou. This sad episode inspires a series of Indian ink drawings, noticed by his mother's lover, the writer Rainer Maria Rilke. The collection devoted to Mitsou is published two years later, in 1921. Balthus never ceases to depict cats, silent companions to his female models, between eroticism and mystery. For him, the cat is a perfect alter ego.

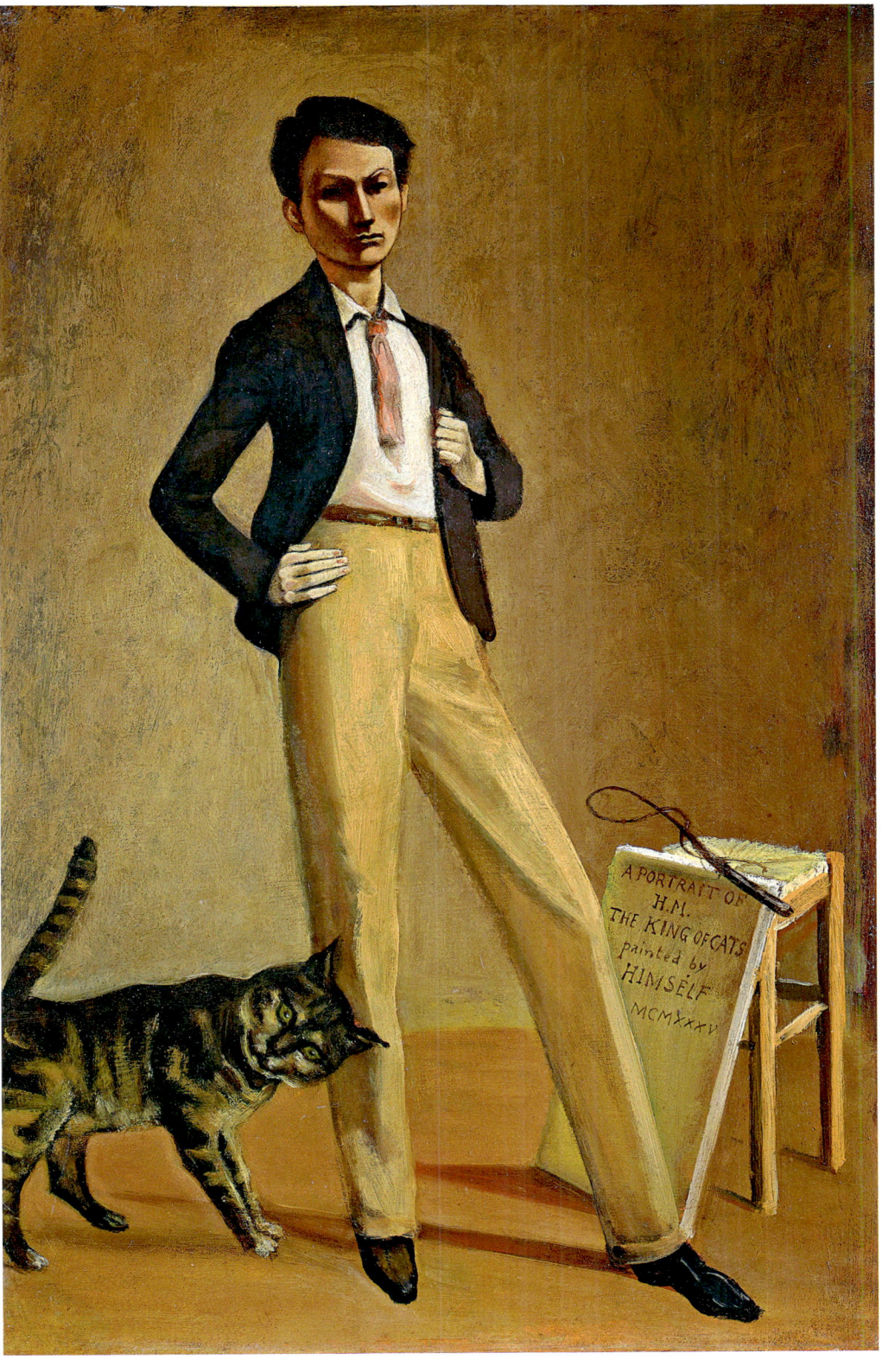

Cat Catching a Bird

1939

The Cat and the War

The Cat and the Bird

Picasso's **cats** are often painted with a certain brutality. **Carnivorous** and **hirsute**, they attack birds, crabs, and crayfish with rage. On the other hand, the **bird** symbolizes **freedom** and **peace**. The famous dove of peace, all white, curved, and delicate, is drawn by Picasso after the Second World War. The dove is a motif that he regularly uses during the 1950s and 1960s.

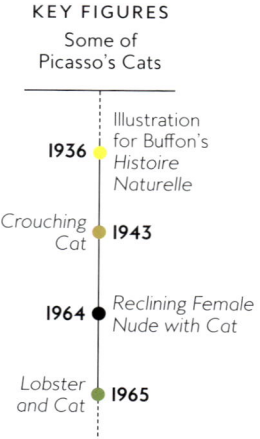

KEY FIGURES
Some of Picasso's Cats

1936 — Illustration for Buffon's *Histoire Naturelle*

Crouching Cat — **1943**

1964 — *Reclining Female Nude with Cat*

Lobster and Cat — **1965**

In the spring of 1939, Picasso is fifty-eight years old. He shares his life with Dora Maar. They follow the events that are pushing Europe towards war. Picasso will never paint the conflict directly, but a distressing and violent atmosphere invades his painting.

The beginning of 1939 is more than bleak. In January, a few days after the death of his mother, Picasso learns that Barcelona had fallen to Franco's regime. At the beginning of April, Franco's dictatorship begins in Spain. On March 15, German troops enter Prague. On April 20, to mark Hitler's fiftieth birthday, a military parade is organized in Berlin; the Waffen-SS are in the lead. Two days later, Picasso paints a *Cat Catching a Bird*. The date April 22, 1939 is scratched into the painting, top left.

On a light background, Picasso depicts a brown and black tabby cat. These colors are no accident. The cat's entire body seems contracted, tense: its back is arched, its white claws grip the ground, while its ears are pointed, and its tail is erect. It seizes a black bird between its fangs. The bird is already dead. Its gaping red wound and open beak are a spectacle both banal and extremely violent. The painter has distributed with economy the three primitive colors of Western culture: black, white, red. The cat's head resembles a Cubist mask. Its expressionless and disturbing eyes are reminiscent of *Les Demoiselles d'Avignon* (*The Young Ladies of Avignon*), painted thirty years earlier.

Picasso rarely paints war and current political events, except in *Guernica* (1937), *The Charnel House* (1945), and *Massacre in Korea* (1951). He explains that he does not look for the subject like a photographer. But he confides: "There is no doubt that the war exists in the paintings that I made then."

"I adore cats that have turned wild, their hair standing on end. They hunt birds, prowl, roam the streets like demons."

Picasso to Brassaï, 1943

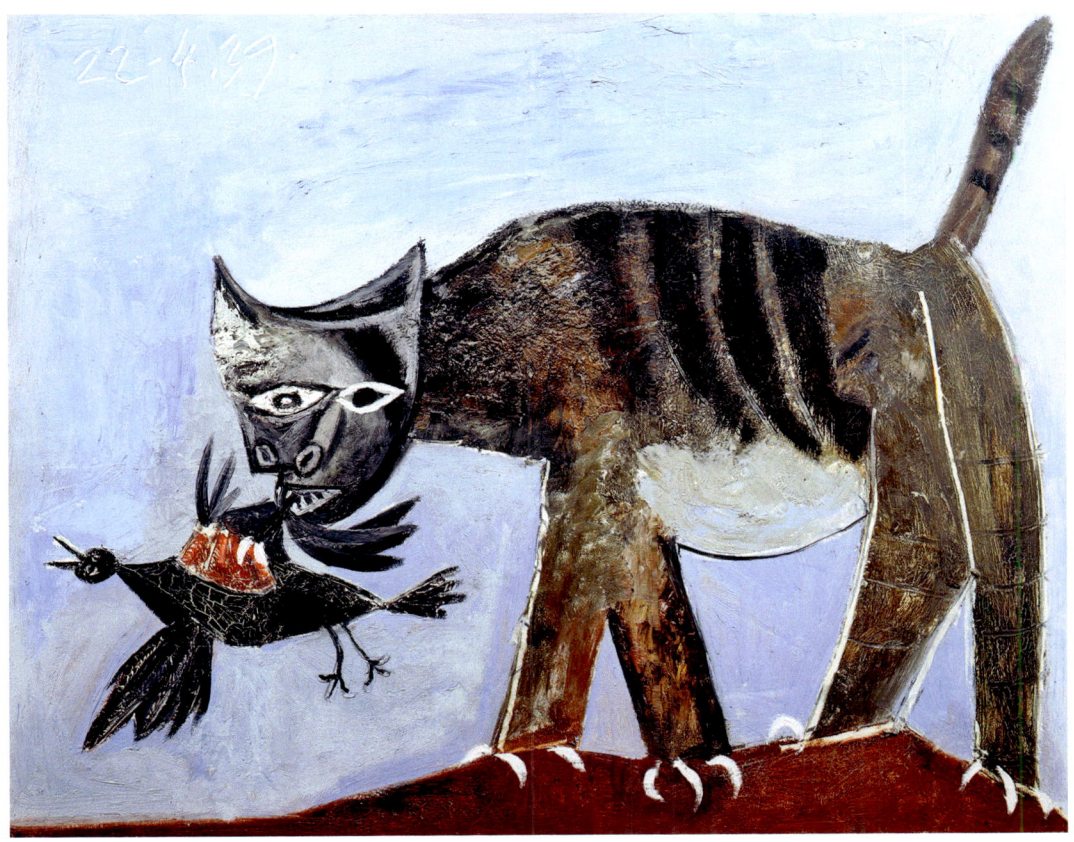

Cat Catching a Bird
(Chat saisissant un oiseau)
Pablo Picasso
1939
Oil on canvas
Musée national Picasso, Paris

The Cat

1951

Straight Cat, Curved Dog

The same year, **Giacometti** created *The Dog*, just as slender but totally different, if not opposite. The hunched old canine is treated with humor and compassion. It swings his tail and floppy ears to the rhythm of its slow walk.

KEY FIGURES
Some Sculpted Cats

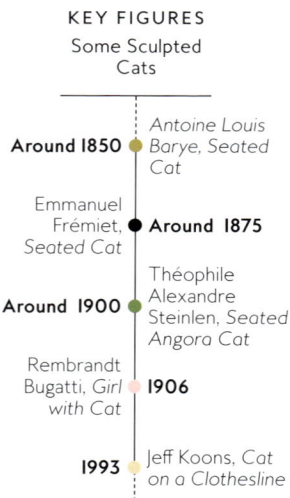

Around 1850 — *Antoine Louis Barye, Seated Cat*

Emmanuel Frémiet, *Seated Cat* — **Around 1875**

Around 1900 — Théophile Alexandre Steinlen, *Seated Angora Cat*

Rembrandt Bugatti, *Girl with Cat* — **1906**

1993 — Jeff Koons, *Cat on a Clothesline*

The Cat
(*Le Chat*)
Alberto Giacometti
1951
Bronze
The Metropolitan Museum of Art, New York

Spinning Feline

Giacometti's slender characters are art icons. The Swiss artist is obsessed by the human figure, and yet, in 1951, he executed three remarkable animal sculptures: a horse, a dog, and a cat.

The starting point for *The Cat* of 1951 was certainly the observation of a real cat, that of Diego Giacometti, Alberto's brother and collaborator. The artist often examined the feline that "passed like a ray of light," sliding its supple predatory form between the objects of the house without ever touching them.

Giacometti does not paint a portrait of a cat but works to render the idea—the quintessence—of the feline, without tenderness or affect. Its slender silhouette advances, silent, its legs following an imaginary line. The shoulder blades are protruded, the tail slightly raised, and the head tensed, its gaze watching for prey. The feline's body is flexible, moving, and perfectly horizontal. This cat is an apparition.

If you squint, it almost looks like an abstract work: two triangles placed on a thick horizontal line—the base, an important part of the work for Giacometti—and connected by another horizontal line. This simplicity reminds us that before his return to figuration in the mid-1930s, Giacometti was not only a surrealist, but also an abstract artist, handling simple geometric shapes and playing with suspensions to find the right balance.

Our cat seems worn out, eaten away by time. It is reminiscent of those Etruscan bronze statuettes discovered rusty and almost crumbly. Giacometti is fascinated by the efficiency and simplicity of ancient forms. How can you not think of a cat mummy when looking at this little round head on a perfectly linear body?

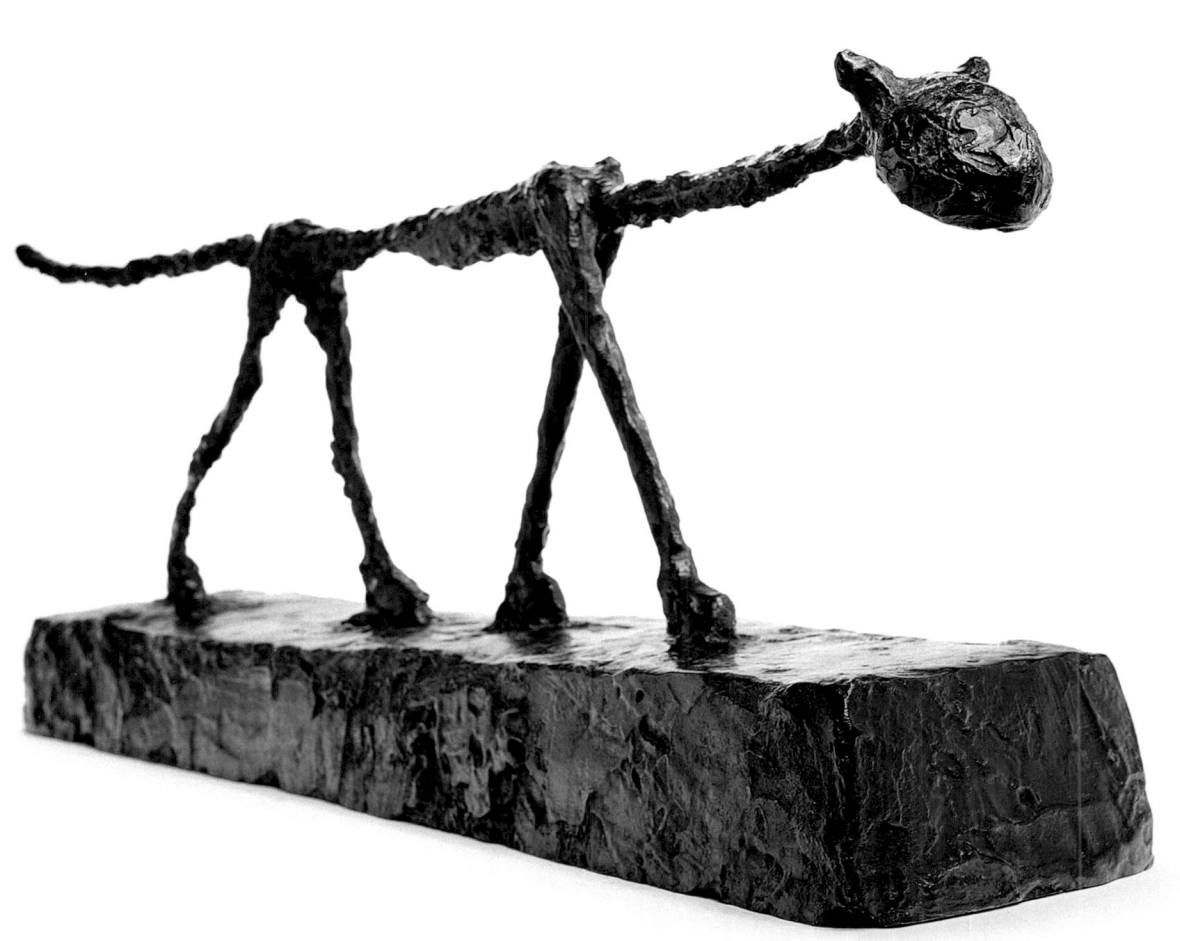

Sam, Yellow Cat

1954

Pop Cat

We all know Andy Warhol, his Campbell's soups, his Marilyn Monroe, his multicolored Mao Zedong, and his multiplied Elvis. But have we ever stopped to focus on his cats?

Sam, a yellow cat with big red eyes, looks at us. Sam is Andy's cat . . . and his mother's. And Sam is not the only one. In the mid-1950s, Andy lives in New York with his mother, Julia, and a couple of cats: Hester and Sam, parents of a string of kittens. The apartment, a two-bedroom on Lexington Avenue, is invaded. There are cats everywhere: in the living room, the bedroom, the bathroom—and apart from Hester, they are all called Sam!

This drawing dates from a little-known but important period: the rise of the king of Pop Art. It bears witness to his offbeat lifestyle. Warhol is a dandy who frequents Upper East Side cafés, but lives with his mom and a multitude of cats. Warhol decorates shop windows of department stores and tries his luck as an illustrator. His cheerful, original drawings make him a household name. He acquires significant fame in the world of advertising and fashion by working for the magazines *Vogue*, *Vanity Fair*, and *The New Yorker*. On the side, he carries out more personal projects: little books he makes for his friends and family. He writes humorous poems, illustrates fake cooking recipes, and draws his cats. His mother copies the texts by hand in her charming curly handwriting.

The 1954 cat lithographs are not a Pop silkscreen, but the principle is in gestation. The cats are drawn in a simple way. They are colored in flat areas of totally fanciful bright colors. Our Sam is lemon yellow. But there are many other Sams: lying down, sitting up, front or sideways, candy pink with green eyes, purple with orange eyes, or blue with yellow eyes.

Warhol or Warhola?

In 1949, Andrew **Warhola**, the son of Slovak immigrants, is twenty-one years old. He arrives in New York and receives his first commission for *Glamour* magazine. The magazine makes a mistake with his name, spelling it without the final "a." From then on, Andy signs **Warhol**.

Warhol in a Few Dates

1949: Arrival in New York
1951: Shoe illustrations for *Harper's Bazaar*
1962: *Campbell's Soup Cans*, *Marilyn Diptych*, and *Triple Elvis*
1963: *Ten Lizes*
1964: Creation of The Factory, his studio
1964: *Flowers*
1972: *Mao Zedong*
1985-1987: *Andy Warhol's Fifteen Minutes*, program on MTV

Sam, Yellow Cat
Andy Warhol
1954
Lithograph
Private collection

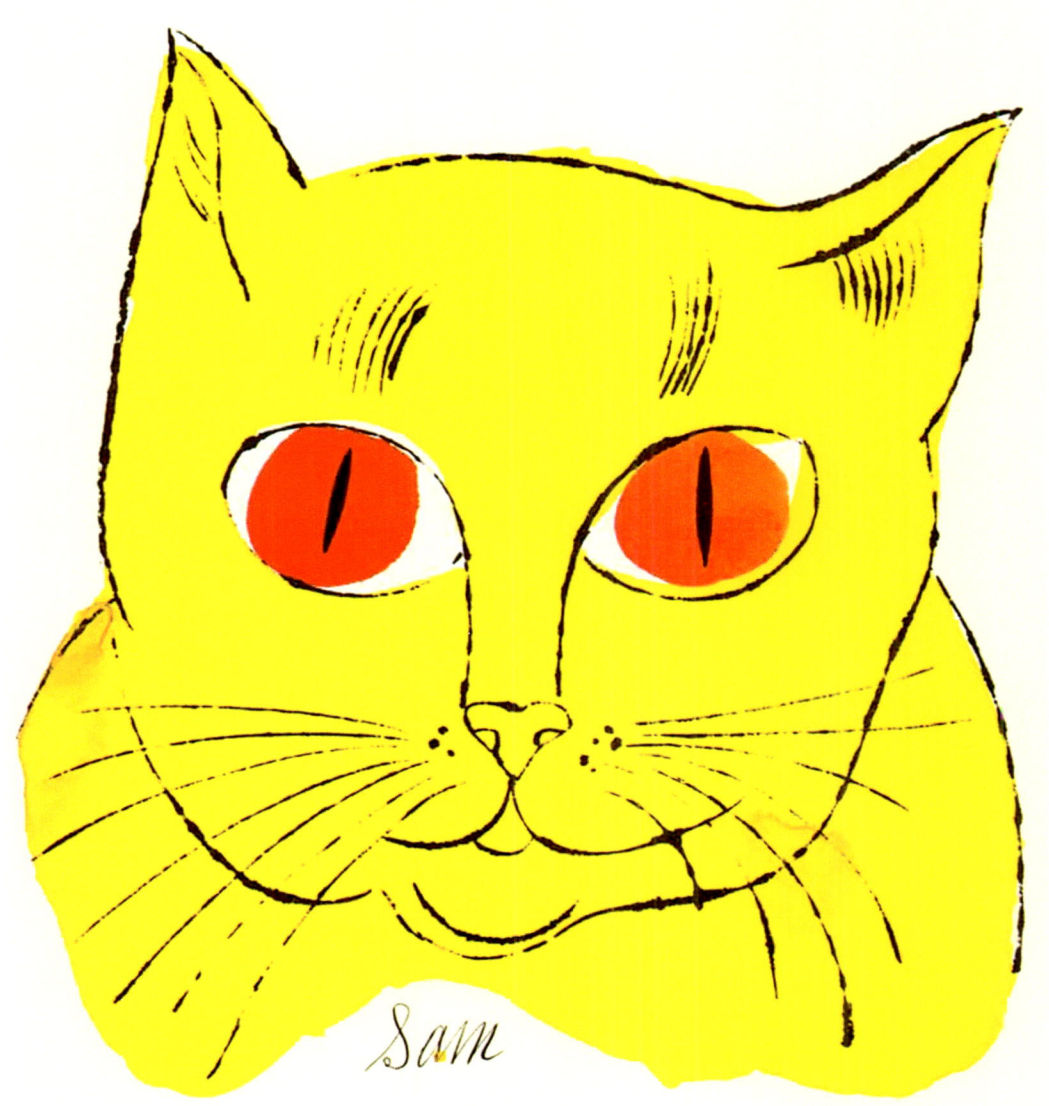

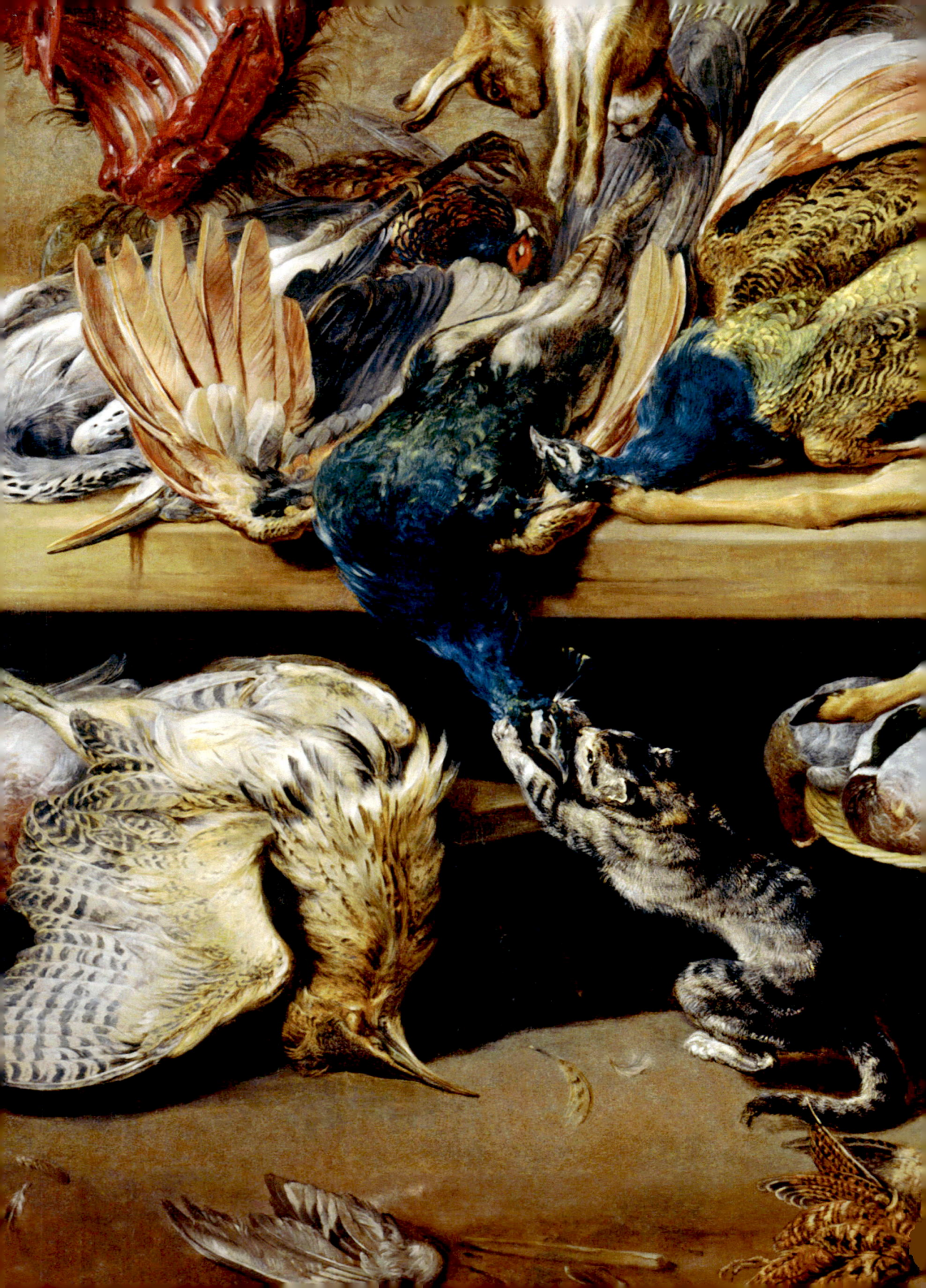

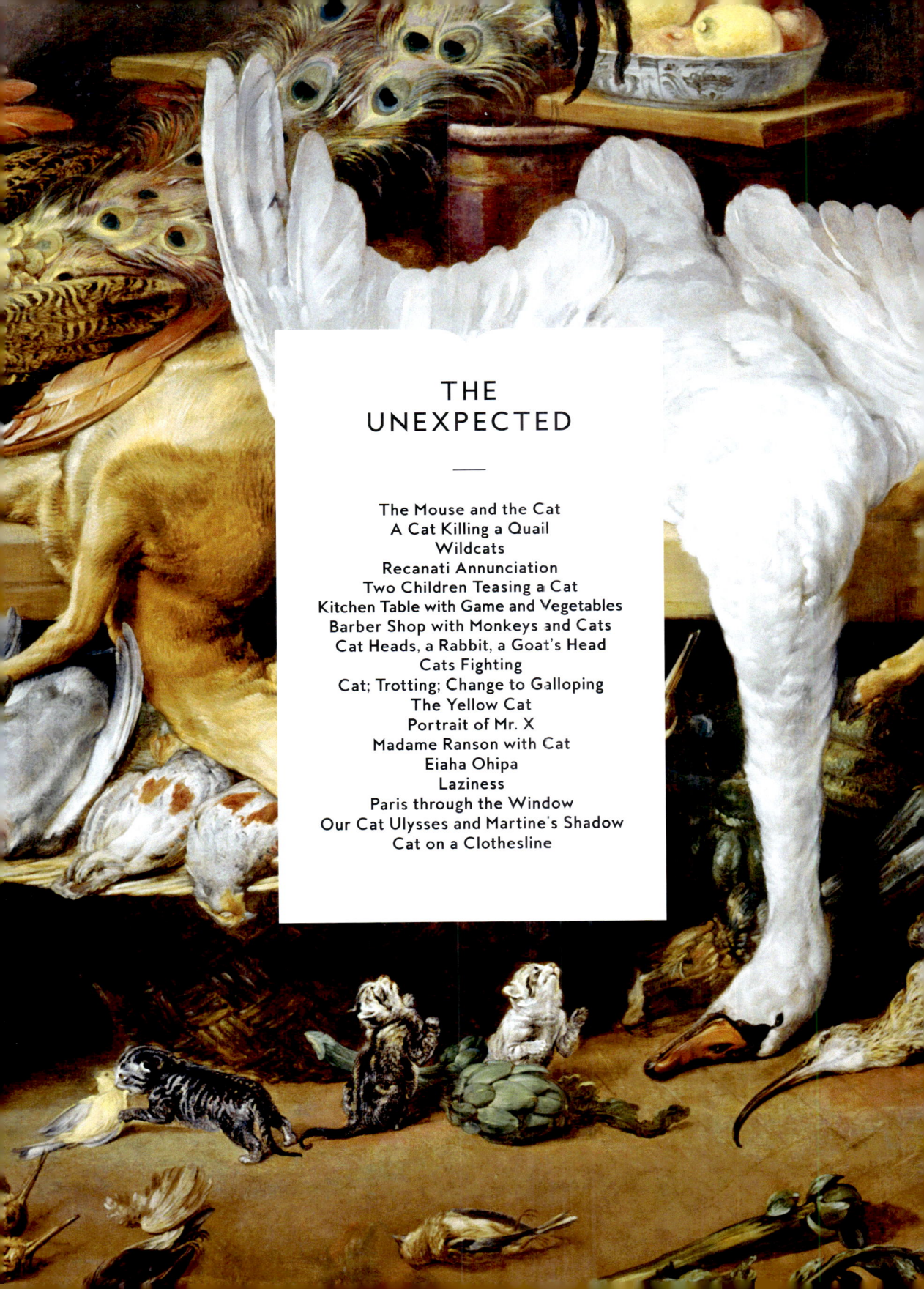

THE
UNEXPECTED

The Mouse and the Cat

16th–11th Century BCE

The Mouse and the Cat
Ostracon from Deir el-Medina
16th–11th century BCE
Limestone
Musées royaux d'Art et d'Histoire, Brussels

Funny Egyptians

Egyptian art is not just about mummies and statuettes of the goddess Bastet; there are also common cats, sometimes drawn with humor.

What is an ostracon? It is a piece of limestone, or more rarely pottery, on which a text or drawing has been written. The ostraca of Deir el-Medina constitute a collection of lively, original works. Their authors are the tomb painters of the Valley of the Kings. These artists, well-versed in the art of drawing, live in the village of Deir el-Medina, not far from the tombs. Ostraca have been discovered in the village, but also near and inside the royal tombs.

Figured ostraca often feature a double black and red line. They can serve as a rough draft for apprentice exercises corrected by their master or as a place for personal artistic expression. The subjects are very varied: realistic or satirical, inspired by nature or poetry, representing men or animals, like this unexpected representation of a mouse lord served by his pet cat.

The inferior mouse that has come to power sits contentedly in front of a table on which appetizing poultry is served. It is dressed in the traditional linen loincloth, the *schenti*. It inhales the sweet scent of a lotus flower and holds a cloth in its other hand. In front of it, its cat servant stands. You can recognize the Egyptian wildcat by its striped coat and high ears. It fans its master with a flabellum, a fan of feathers or leaves attached to a long handle.

This ostracon is not unique. There are other examples of mice being served by cats. Is it a fable transmitted by oral tradition and forgotten? Does the image have a satirical significance, a criticism of the society made up of masters, servants, and slaves? The mystery remains.

"The limits of art are not reached; no artist ever possesses that perfection to which he should aspire."

Ptahhotep, vizier of the 5th Dynasty

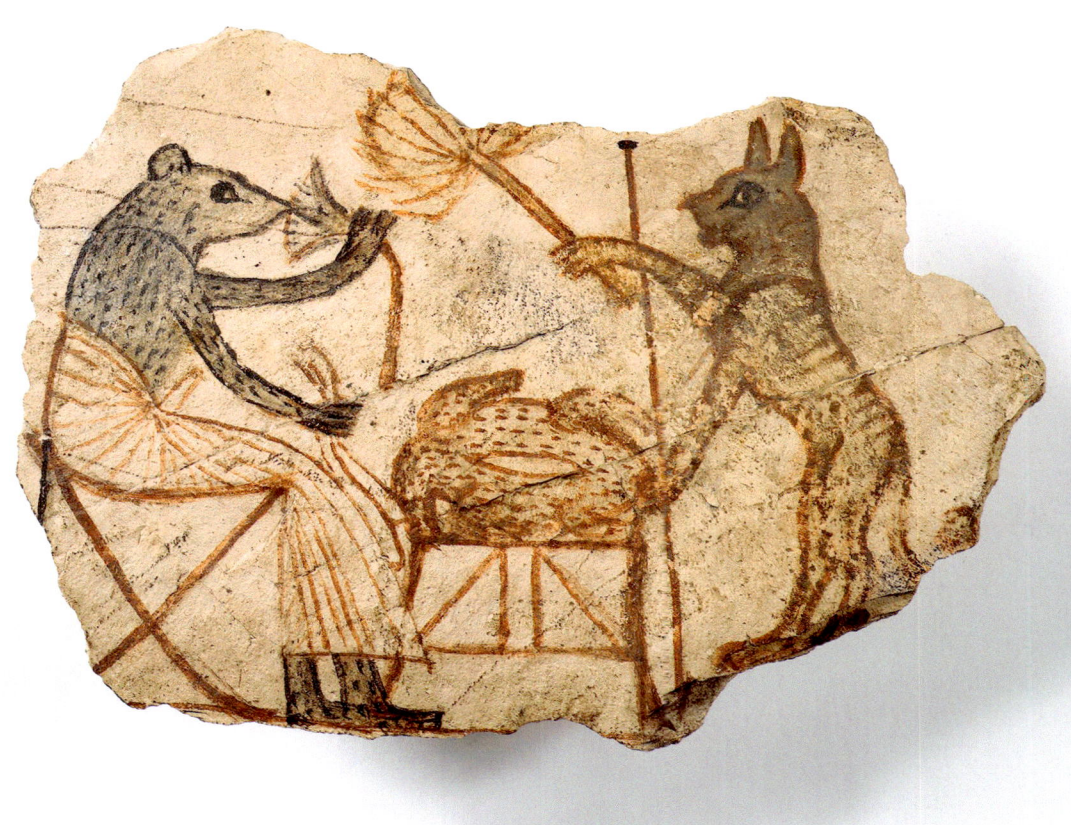

A Cat Killing a Quail

2nd Century BCE

And among the Greeks?

The cat is almost absent. However, the first Westerner to mention it was the historian **Herodotus**, in 5th century BCE, during his trip to Egypt. In Greece, the favorite pet is the bird. Cats are therefore not welcome among them. When it comes to eradicating rodents, there's no need for a cat: the **Greeks** domesticated the weasel.

Pixels Before Their Time

Mosaic is the Roman art par excellence. To create drawings with soft lines and minute details, the Romans used **tesserae** (small cubes of stone, marble, or glass paste) measuring only a few millimeters. This technique is known as *opus vermiculatum*. Depending on the size and cut of the tesserae, there is also *opus tessellatum* (larger), opus sectile (one tile forms the entire piece).

Bad Flaws

Did the Romans not know about this feline, or was it unloved to the point of not being represented?

Greek and Roman artists depicted big cats—panthers, cheetahs, and leopards—on vases, mosaics, and frescoes. On the other hand, it is difficult to identify domesticated cats. Archaeologists often hesitate: are they puppies, weasels, lynxes, or cats?

This Cat Killing a Quail is one of the only examples known from Roman antiquity. It comes from the floor of the second atrium of the House of the Faun, a Pompeii residence of immense decorative richness. Above, a cat seizes a quail. Below, ducks, fish, and shellfish are juxtaposed. The cat catches the bird with its claws out. Aggressive and wild: we are indeed facing a cat from Roman antiquity.

At the time, the feline is little appreciated. It is rare in towns and farms. Attracted by birds and rodents, it lives alongside humans without being domesticated. In his treatise on animals, Aristotle says of the weasel that it "preys on birds like the cat." And Aesop, long before him, already featured in his *Fables* the cat "devouring" poultry, rats, or mice. The image of the cat, aggressive and carnivorous, is all the more negative as it is associated by the Romans with unbridled sexuality and therefore reprehensible. Herodotus, Aristotle, and Plutarch reference the cat for its sexual behavior and high fertility.

Cunning, supple, sexual . . . all the negative qualities of the cat begin to be associated with those of the woman, and the female sex is compared to a cat. Plutarch tells us that cats love the good smell of perfume like women. Here is a lexicon in the making that is sure to have a bright future ahead of it!

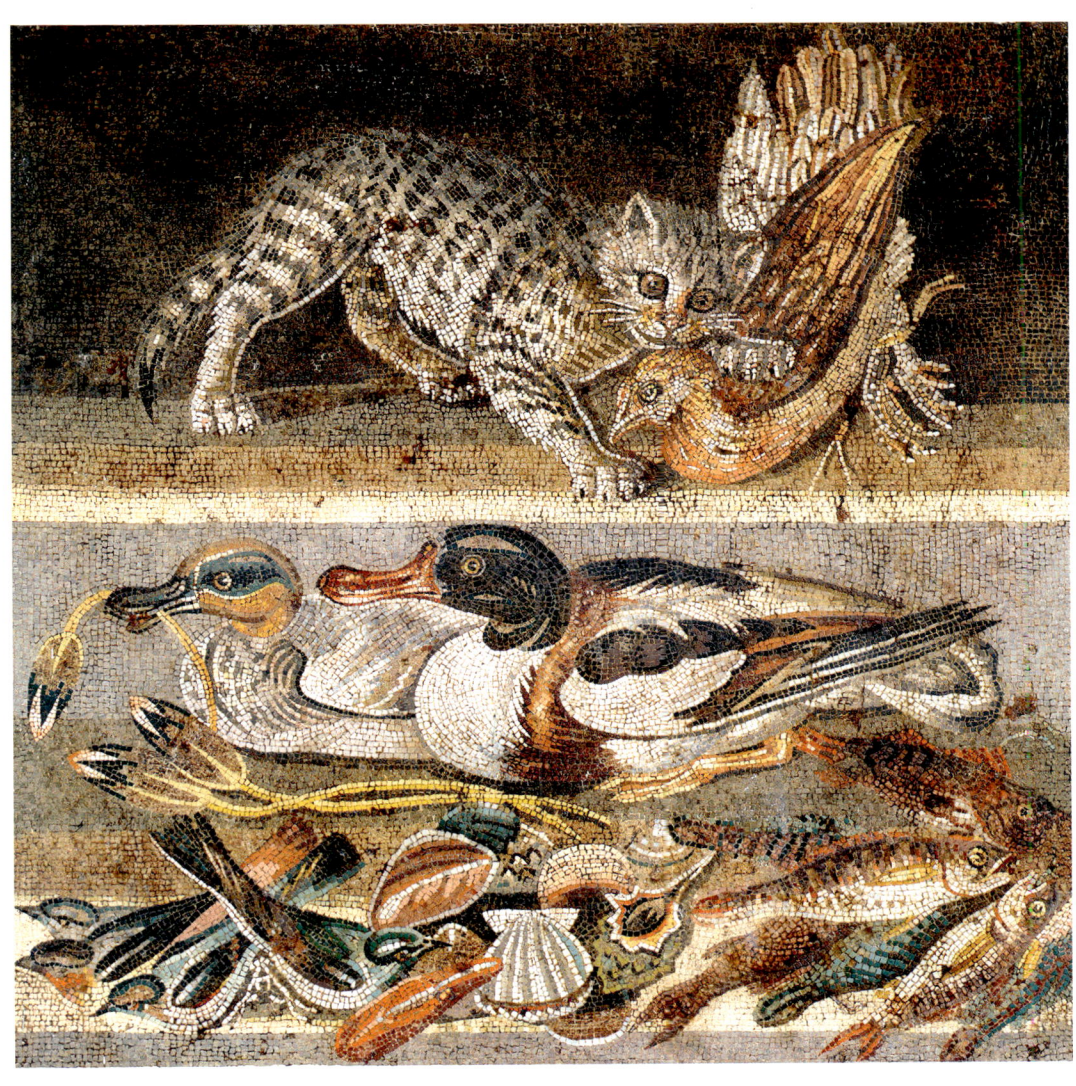

A Cat Killing a Quail
2ⁿᵈ century BCE
Mosaic
Museo Archeologico Nazionale,
Naples

Wildcats

1387-1388

Medieval Wildcats

Hunting in the Middle Ages

A leisure activity practiced by all social groups, hunting is a prestigious **entertainment** for the nobles, who hunt with falcons, hawks, and hounds, but it is above all a **moral activity** that keeps man away from sin and idleness.

The Medieval Bestiary
———

Real or legendary, animals are loaded with **symbols**, often **religious**, that can vary depending on the context. The **favored**: bear, lion, deer, ox, eagle, pelican, dove, unicorn, phoenix. The **unfavored**: pig, fox, cat, snake, wolf, dragon, wild donkey.

Wildcats in *The Hunting Book*
(*Chats sauvages*, dans *Le Livre de chasse*)
Gaston Phébus
1387-1388
Vellum, miniatures, decorated letters
Bibliothèque nationale de France, Paris

It was not until the Middle Ages that the cat spread throughout the countryside. It is allowed on farms and in homes, even in the bedroom, although it remains a solitary animal. In this rare 14th-century illumination, Gaston Phébus engages himself in the observation of the wildcat.

Cats have massive bodies and strong legs. Some are dark gray, while others, spotted, almost look like leopards, to which they are compared by the author. They engage in various activities: some climb a tree, one licks its fur while another catches a small rodent. Some finally lounge, lying down or curling up in their den.

In the Middle Ages, the cat was more highly regarded, but it did not yet have domestic status: we are far from the tomcat purring in front of the fireplace. Its relationship with man remains distant and ambivalent. It is tolerated but remains a worker whose mission is to eat mice. It rarely has a first name, is not a playmate, and often lives semi-wanderingly. The cat is, of course, not fed, otherwise it would no longer be hungry and would not rid the house of rodents.

At this time, cats appear in the margins of manuscripts. If they are often drawn in a rather grotesque manner, it is because they are considered unsightly. "Having a cat's nose" is a serious physical defect. And when Chrétien de Troyes, in *Perceval: The Story of the Grail*, uses this comparison to describe a young lady, he adds that there was "never a creature so ugly even in the bowels of Hell."

The illumination by Gaston Phébus is exceptional. This lord of the Foix region, an outstanding hunter, is a great bibliophile. He is the first to describe animals in their natural environment. He thus offers zoological plates ahead of their time.

mar, il ne se ole mie tant aua
turer le iour comme il fait.
car il ne seet ne puet fuir. Il
vit plus de dormir que dautre
chose. Ilz sont une foiz lan leur
chiens comme regnars. et les
font dedanz les folles comme
regnars. Quant on les chasse
ilz se deffendent fort. et ont
leur morsur venimeuse co
me regnart. Encore se deffen
dent ilz plusfort que ne fait
le regnart. Cest la beste du mõ

de qui plus acquieust greffe
dedanz. et cest pour le long
dormir quil fait. et son sanc
porte medecine comme cellui
du regnart. On dit q un enfant
qui onques nauroit chausse
sollers. si les premiers quil
chausse sont de pel de traisson.
il garira les chevaulx du faut
sil monte sus. mar ie ne lafer
me mie. sa char ne vault rien
a mengier nõ fait celle du reg
nart. nõ fait celle du loup.

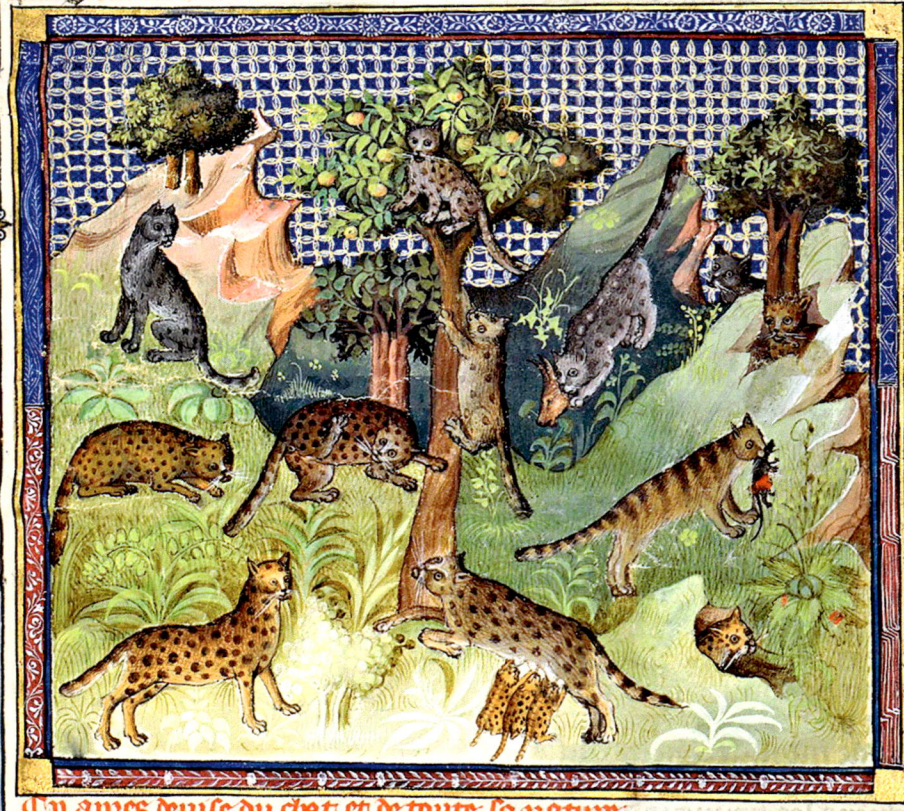

Recanati Annunciation

1527-1528

What Does the Bible Say?

Although Christianity often associated the cat with the **Devil** in the **Middle Ages**, it is never mentioned in the **Bible**. Its presence is an invention of the artists. In **Islam**, on the other hand, the cat has enjoyed a very **positive** connotation since medieval times.

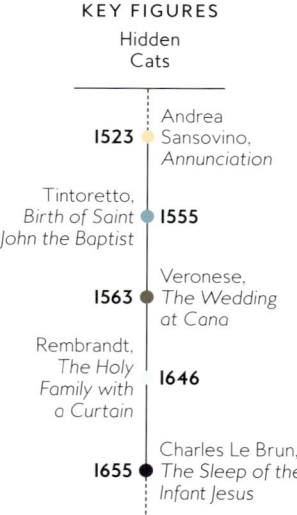

KEY FIGURES
Hidden
Cats

1523 Andrea Sansovino, *Annunciation*

Tintoretto, *Birth of Saint John the Baptist* **1555**

1563 Veronese, *The Wedding at Cana*

Rembrandt, *The Holy Family with a Curtain* **1646**

1655 Charles Le Brun, *The Sleep of the Infant Jesus*

The Recanati Annunciation
(*Annunciazione di Recanati*)
Lorenzo Lotto
1527-1528
Oil on canvas
Museo Civico di Villa Colloredo
Mels, Recanati

Run for Your Life!

In 1527, painting an Annunciation was very traditional. However, one detail here is very unusual: right in the center of the painting, a cat runs away.

The angel Gabriel carries a lily—a symbol of purity—and lands beside the Virgin to announce that she is to be the mother of Christ. Mary, immersed in her reading, is surprised and even frightened. Above, God the Father splits the clouds. The triangular composition is clever. Hands, looks, and colors guide our eye. Gabriel, in blue, extends his hand to God the Father, in red. God extends both hands toward Mary, dressed in red and blue. God and the angel look at the Virgin who looks at us. Facing us, she opens her hands in astonishment. In the center of this colorful trio, a little tabby cat leaps. He is there to make the link between the two sides of the painting: the human on the left (Mary, the room, her belongings) and the sacred on the right (Gabriel, God, the clouds).

The cat's frozen momentum creates the impression of a freeze frame. Time, symbolized by the hourglass on the stool, seems suspended. The presence of a cat in an Annunciation is uncommon. It reinforces the effect of surprise. The angel has just landed, his hair and drapery still in motion. He disturbed the feline, which leaps away, looks at him with its suspicious little eyes.

During the Renaissance, the cat acquired the status of a domestic animal and its presence here reinforced the feeling of proximity. Many everyday details are painted by Lotto: the coat hook with Mary's clothes, the shelf with books and the candleholder, the four-poster bed, emblematic of the intimacy of the home. Some historians think that the presence of the cat represents a break with conventional paintings, others think it evokes the image of the Devil who flees from the angel.

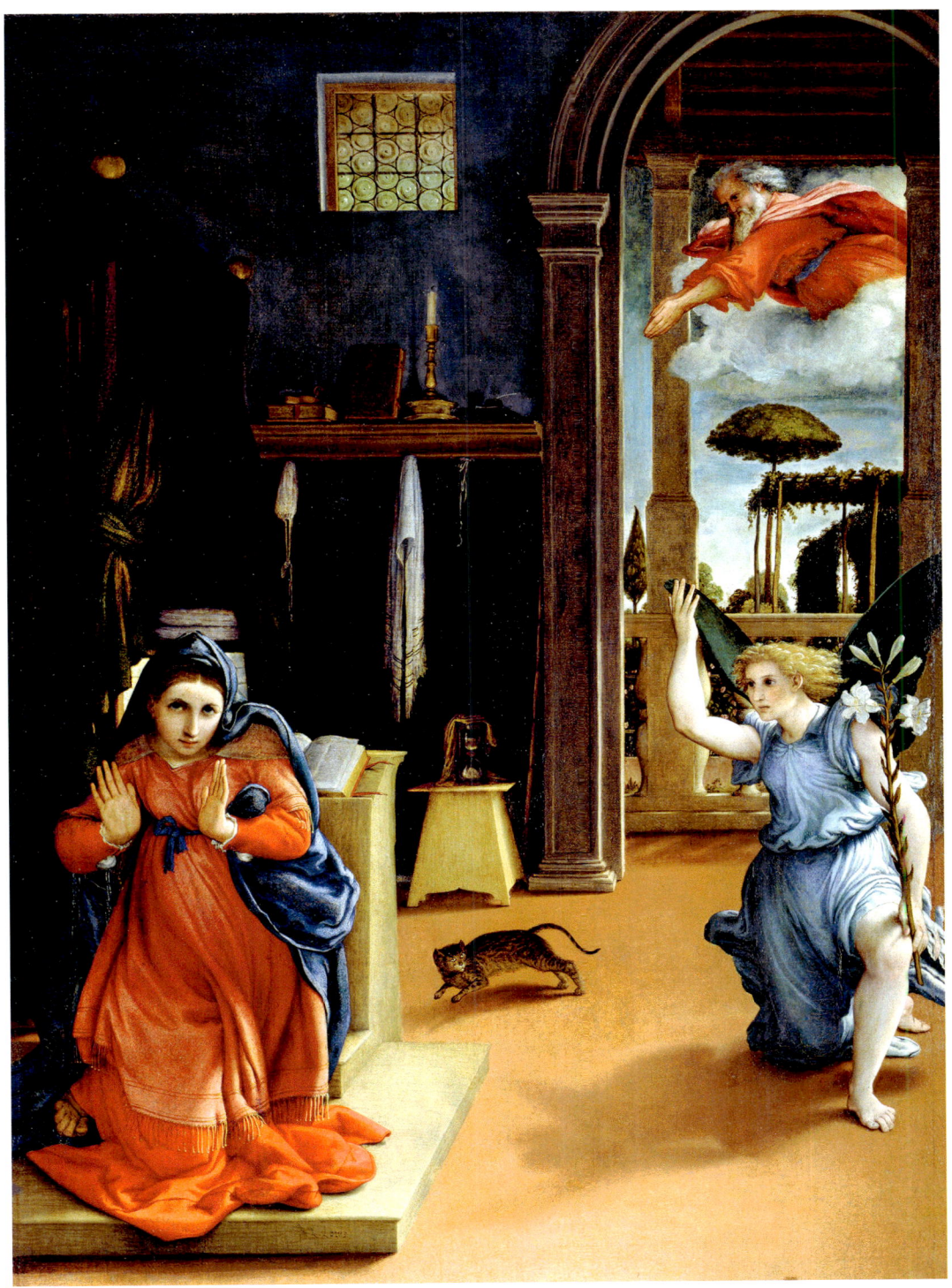

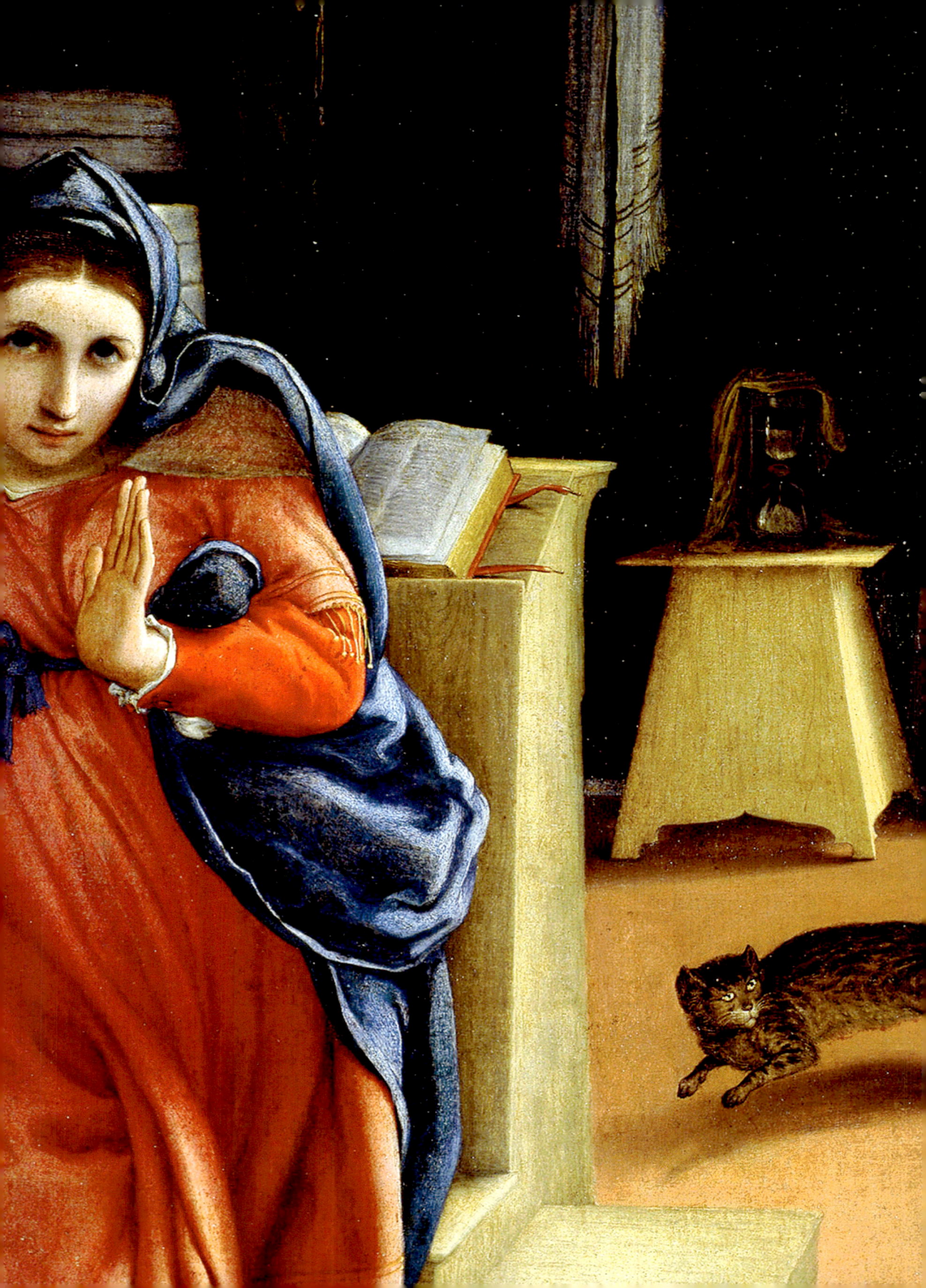

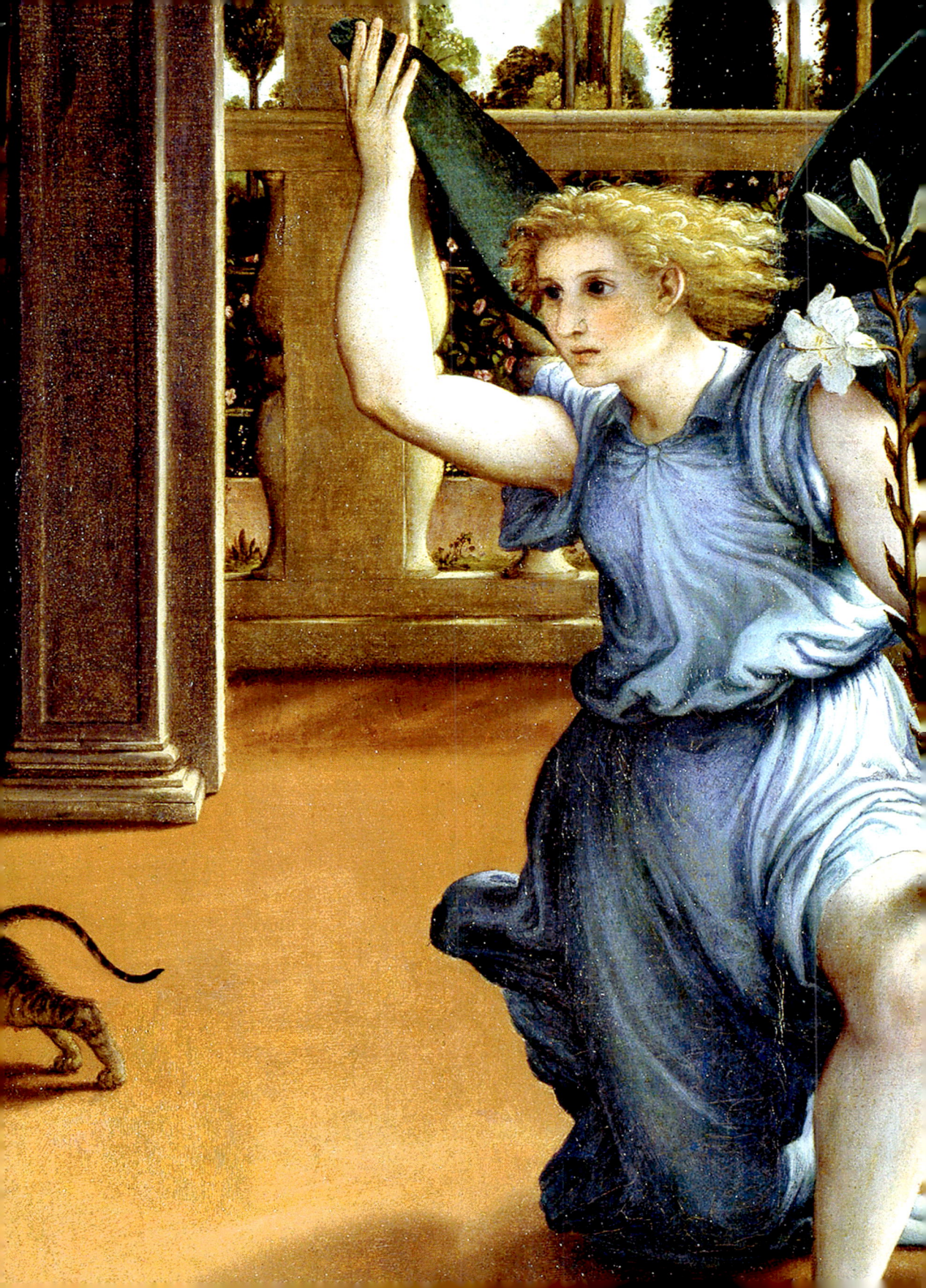

Two Children Teasing a Cat

Around 1590

Don't Wake the Sleeping Cat

Martyr Cats

During the early modern period and throughout Europe, cats are frequent objects of **violent folk rituals**. This is the case during the carnival season, where cats take on a sexual dimension, as well as at Midsummer: cats are burned or locked in a bag to drown them.

Poor Crustacean

It is not unusual to come across crustaceans in allegorical or vanitas painting in the 17th century. Whether it is a crab or a crayfish, the crustacean is synonymous with **disloyalty** or **moral deviance** . . . because it moves sideways.

Two Children Teasing a Cat
(Due bambini molestano un gatto)
Annibale Carracci
Around 1590
Oil on canvas
The Metropolitan Museum of Art,
New York

Why are two children trying to pinch the ear of a cat with a crustacean? This enigmatic painting is attributed to Annibale Carracci, one of the most astonishing minds of the Baroque era.

Two kids are having fun with a cat lying quietly on a table. The eldest holds a crawfish in his hand. He has already placed a claw around the cat's ear, but the cat retracts, growling and narrowing its eyes. This skit of animal torture provokes laughter from the little girl . . . but there is no doubt that after being pinched, the cat will scratch the hand unconsciously placed in front of it.

In the 17th century, the cat is still an ambivalent animal. Increasingly accepted, it remains attached to the Devil and witches in popular culture. Cats were tortured or killed during certain European entertainments until the 18th century. That said, the attitude of the children here is reprehensible, and the cat will come down hard.

A moral reading of the work is permitted: a bad or imprudent action will always be punished. This theme is not an invention of Annibale Carracci. There are several paintings from the same period with children being bitten or pinched by an animal—*Boy Bitten by a Lizard* (Caravaggio, 1594), *Asdrubale Bitten by a Crawfish* (Sofonisba Anguissola, 1554). Like Caravaggio, Carracci seeks to shake up conventions. He wants to move away from sophisticated and mannerist art. He is interested in studying from nature and paints with a lively and spontaneous touch. His ceiling in the gallery of the Palazzo Farnese in Rome will become a reference and one of the models for the Hall of Mirrors in Versailles.

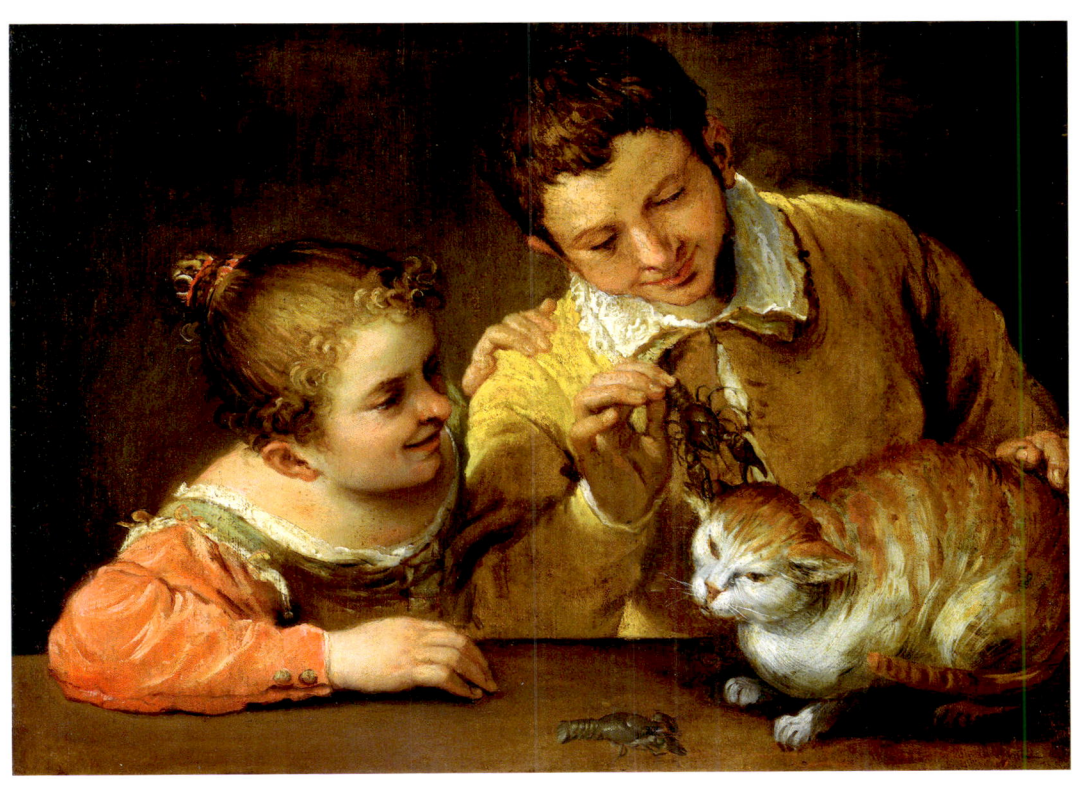

"Young cats are gay, vivacious, and frolicsome, and if nothing was to be apprehended from their claws, would afford excellent amusement for children."

Buffon, *Histoire Naturelle*

Kitchen Table with Game and Vegetables

Around 1630

Little Thieves

The ultimate kitchen pilferer, the cat is often associated with gluttony. And Frans Snyders, a specialist in tables overflowing with victuals, enlivens his compositions with hungry little felines.

In a courtyard, an abundance of victuals piles up on a heavy wooden table. Two deer frame a swan whose head falls to the ground. A wading bird, peacocks, and a pheasant complete the display. Rabbits, partridges, and roosters hang high. Small game is stored under the table, next to the artichokes.

Under a wicker basket filled with ducks, snipe, and other small birds, three gray kittens are busy. They are tiny and reinforce the monumental aspect of the game. The most gifted has managed to catch a yellow bird and crunches into it. The others meow towards the basket, their noses in agitation. The gourmands are accompanied by their mother, a tabby cat attacking a peacock's head. Their agitation doesn't seem to bother the placid little dog sleeping in a ball not far away.

Snyders brilliantly paints animals, both living and dead, particularly textures and materials. You almost have the impression that you can touch the soft feathers of the white swan or the short hair of the deer. The abundance of the stall reflects the wealth of its city. The port of Antwerp is a major economic and artistic capital. Painters are numerous and commissions are pouring in. Churches, nobles, bourgeoisie, guilds, merchants . . . all wanting paintings to decorate their interiors. Painters specialize—some are gifted with figures, others with landscapes or animals. Snyders was a household name. Rubens called on him to paint the animals in his compositions. King Philip IV of Spain commissioned works for his hunting lodge near Madrid.

Spanish Belgium

Catholic Flanders, or Spanish Netherlands, corresponds to present-day **Belgium**. The region's capital was **Brussels**, and its main port was **Antwerp**. It was not independent, but under the dominion of the Habsburg Spanish kings.

Cooking a Peacock

The peacock was eaten by the elite from antiquity to the 17th century. It is especially appreciated for its **beauty**: with its feathers, it forms an **extravagant dish**. Herons and swans were cooked in the Middle Ages and until the 17th century. They are then replaced by smaller birds: pigeons, chickens, and capons.

"The good apostle, Clapperclaw,
Then laid on each a well-arm'd paw,
And both to an agreement brought,
By virtue of his tusked jaw."

Jean de La Fontaine, "The Cat, the Weasel, and the Little Rabbit" from _Fables_

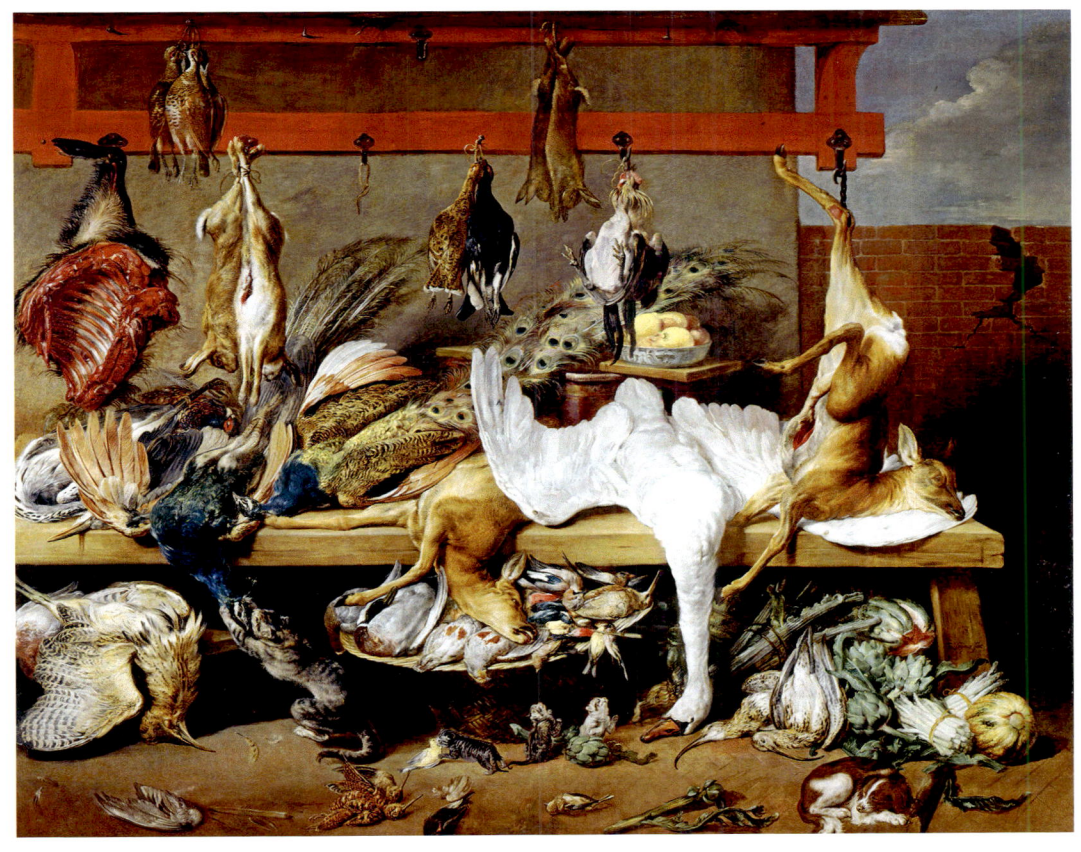

Kitchen Table with Game and Vegetables
(Table de cuisine avec gibier et légumes)
Frans Snyders
Around 1630
Oil on wood
Musée des Beaux-Arts, Lyon

Barber Shop with Monkeys and Cats
Around 1650–1670

A Tale of Monkeys

Singerie is a genre that originated in Flemish painting in the 16th century. **Comic scenes** with monkeys dressed up and evolving in a human environment became very popular in the 17th and 18th centuries. Cats accompany them in several works by the Teniers brothers: The Cat Concert, Monkeys Styling Cats, and so on.

Did You Say Copper?

In the 16th century, alongside with the development of engraving, **Northern European** artists come up with the idea of painting on copper plates. The medium is appreciated for its smooth surface, which allows for fine **detail** and a **glossy** finish close to the original enamel.

A Haircut?

Here's an amazing barbershop. The barbers are monkeys and the customers are cats! A singerie typical of Flemish painting, teeming with amusing and instructive details.

The living room is warmed by a small brazier. A covered ginger cat is sitting on an armchair. It looks at itself in a mirror with satisfaction. Around him, two gray and white monkeys are combing its hair, dutifully trimming its whiskers and ear hairs. Other cats enter, wait, or settle in. A monkey is busy unhooking a copper basin using a pole. Next to it are the barber's tools: razors, scissors, shaving brushes, double combs, and bottles of lotion.

Another heats a white sheet on a copper basin. Two cat customers wait their turn, seated on a chest. One of them looks at us. It has a broken leg in a sling. Near the window, a delighted gray cat holds a basin of hot water and is about to be shaved by a brown monkey with a mischievous smile. A "cat lord" enters, wearing a musketeer's hat and a red cape. It is reminiscent of Puss in Boots.

This image is not taken from Perrault's fairy tale, which would be written some thirty years later. It's a painting on copper, barely seven by eleven inches, created for a lover of antics. This genre, of which the painter Abraham Teniers and his brother were specialists, was very much in vogue in the 17th century.

In this barbershop, the monkeys are busy and the cats are admiring each other. In short, there are the mischievous merchants on one side and the self-satisfied bourgeois on the other. But aren't animals the best way to talk about human life?

76

"If monkeys could reach the point of being bored, they could turn into human beings."
Goethe

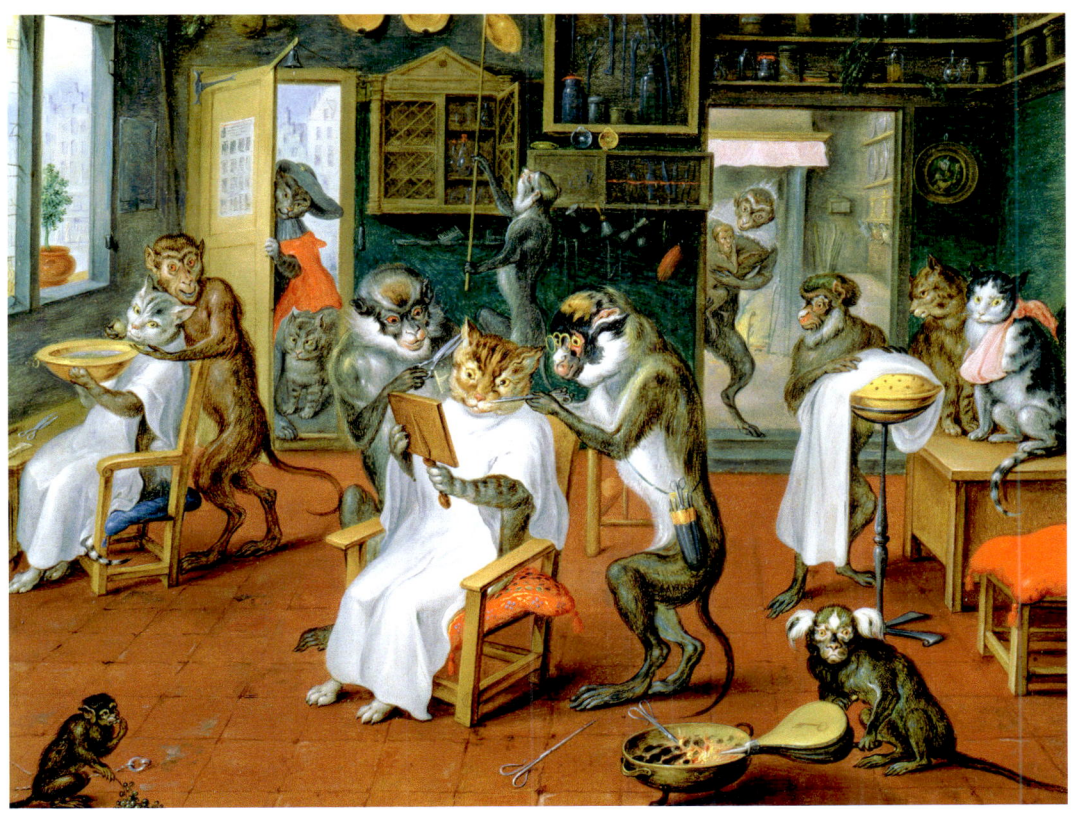

Barber Shop with Monkeys and Cats
(Barbierstube mit affen und katzen)
Abraham Teniers
Around 1650–1670
Oil on copper
Kunsthistorisches Museum, Vienna

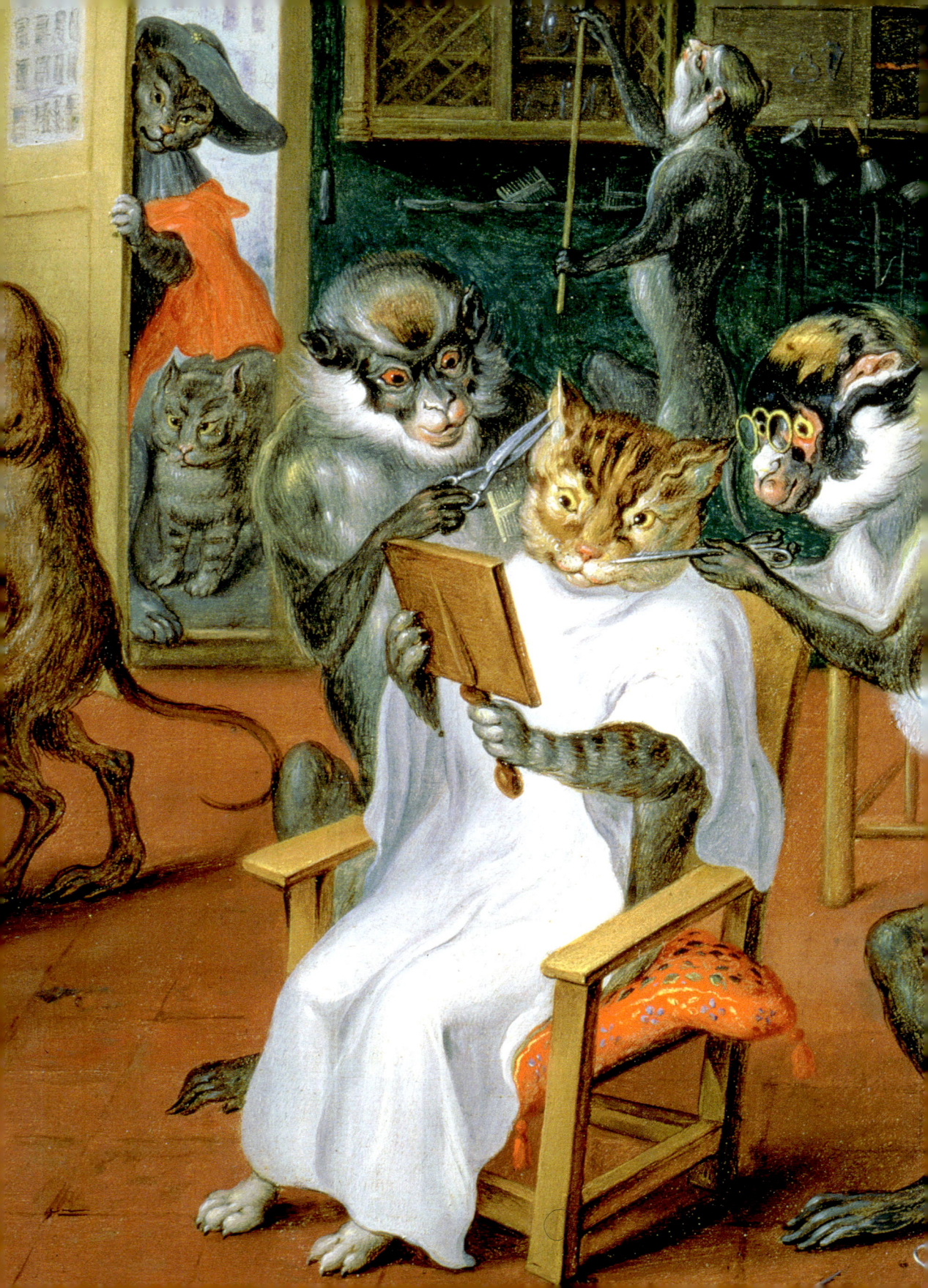

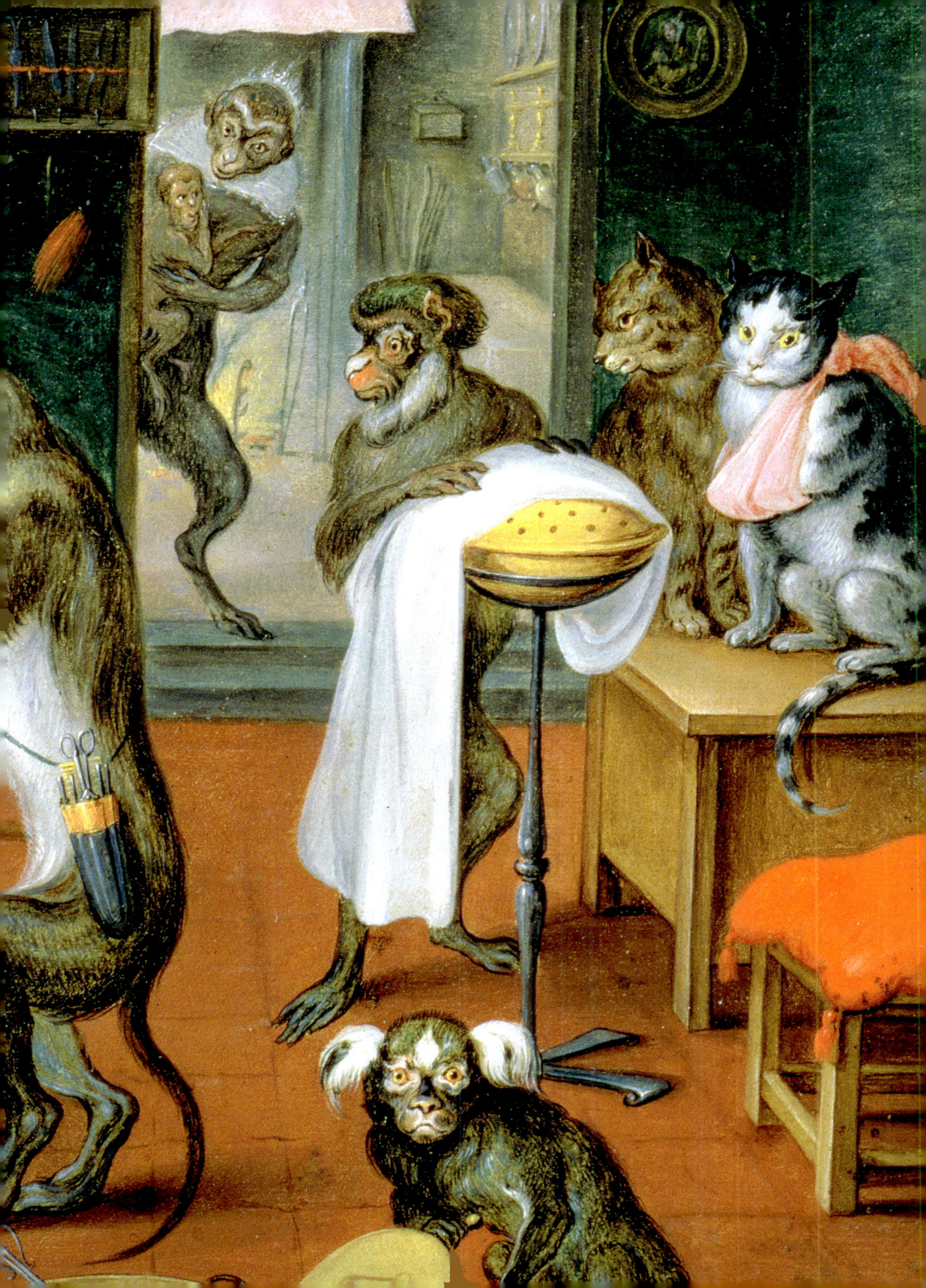

Cat Heads, a Rabbit, a Goat's Head

Around 1670

Prestigious Tapestries

Created under Henry IV in Paris, the royal **Gobelins Manufactory** grows to unprecedented proportions under Louis XIV thanks to Minister Colbert. The factory produces hundreds of pieces for furnishing castles and diplomatic gifts. Its reputation is international.

The Versailles Zoo
———

A place of entertainment that has now disappeared, the **Royal Menagerie** of Versailles was created by Louis XIV. Around a pavilion, seven enclosures housed **exotic animals**. Under Louis XV, there was even a rhinoceros.

Cat Heads, a Rabbit, a Goat's Head
(*Têtes de chats, un lapin, une tête de chèvre*)
Pieter Boel
Around 1670
Oil on canvas
Musée des Beaux-Arts, Alençon

Truer than Life

To produce tapestries for King Louis XIV, the Gobelins Manufactory calls on the best artists in France and Europe. Everyone has their own specialty. Pieter Boel excels in rendering animals.

Here is a cat that meows, yawns, and moves, as realistic as a photograph. And yet, we are at the end of the 17th century. The painter Pieter Boel, a specialist in animals and still lifes, observes this cat from four different angles. He also paints it sitting in the corner of the canvas, accompanied by another feline. Below, a rabbit and a goat's head complete these life studies. In the 17th century, it is not surprising to see cats associated with farm animals, as they were the preferred domestic animal in rural homes, where they hunted rodents.

Boel studies movements and postures by changing points of view. He captures them as spontaneously as possible. He also analyzes and succeeds in rendering the texture of the hair with his rapid, brushed strokes. This rare ability to depict animals in action was noticed by Charles Le Brun, director of The Académie Royale de Peinture et de Sculpture (Academy of Painting and Sculpture) and the Gobelins Manufactory.

At Gobelins the finest tapestries are designed and woven for the Louvre and Versailles castles. Le Brun, who trains artists and spots talent, hires Boel. He paints animals and plants, which are then reproduced in tapestry borders. The Antwerp painter observes everyday animals: cats, dogs, birds, and game. His talents open the doors to the Royal Menagerie of Versailles. There, he has the rare privilege of observing exotic animals. He draws and paints animals for Le Brun that are little known to other artists of the time: monkeys, a lion, a camel, ostriches, parrots, a lynx, and even a cassowary!

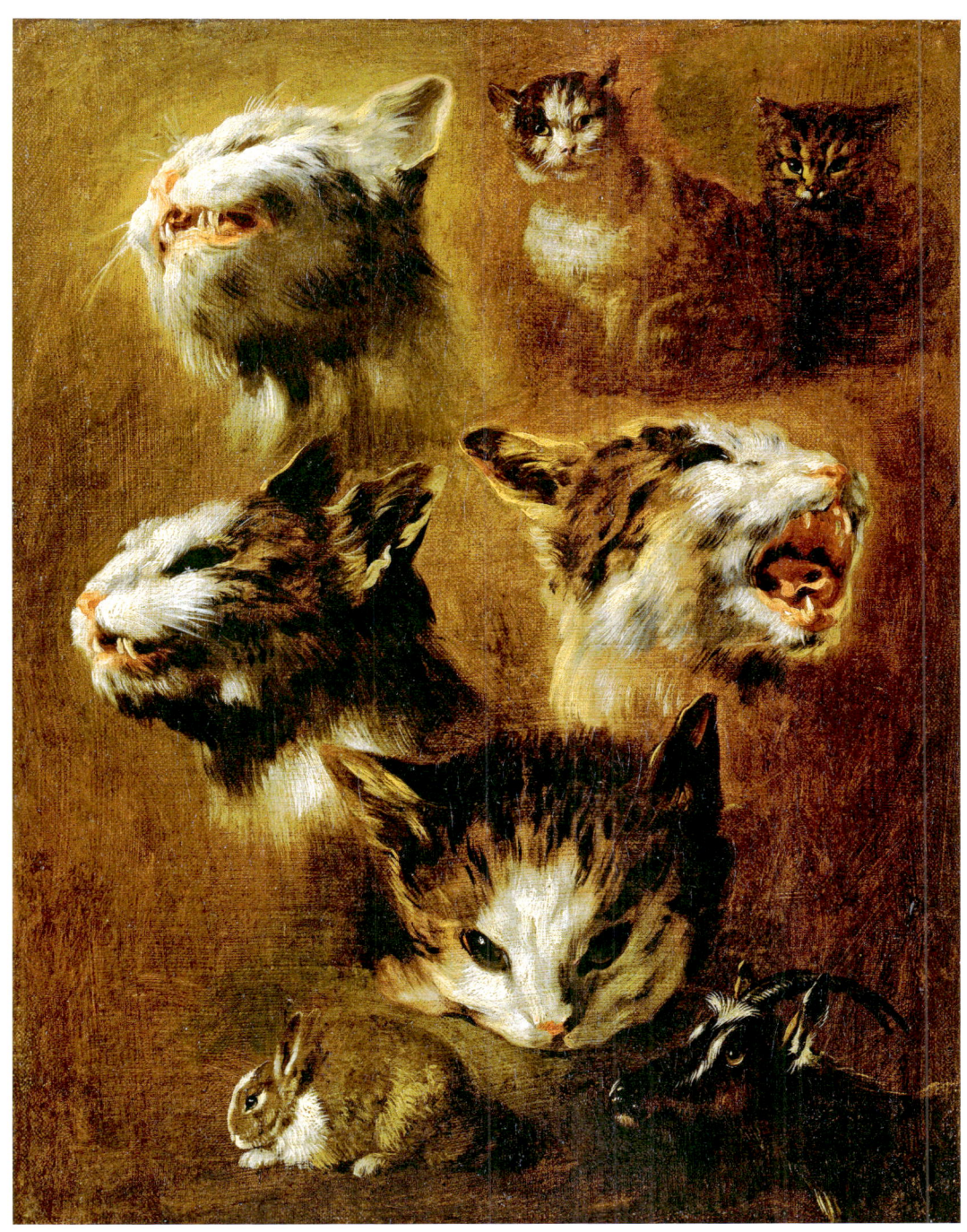

Cats Fighting

Around 1786–1787

Claws Out

Unclassifiable painter, precursor of dark romanticism, Francisco de Goya was a painter at the Spanish court in his youth. His themes are often unusual, as in this *Cats Fighting*.

Two cats face each other on a brick wall. The light is uncertain: is it dawn or dusk? On the dark side, the black cat; on the side where light shines, the gray cat. The felines confront each other, bending their backs and lowering their ears. The black cat, retreating slightly, seems to have lost the game. He has a frightened look and drooping whiskers. We can almost hear the meows of the gray cat, which opens its mouth wide to reveal its sharp little fangs.

This long and narrow work is a preparatory drawing for a tapestry intended to adorn the top of a door in the dining room of the Royal Palace of El Pardo, near Madrid. The location of the tapestry explains the slight low angle: we'll have to pass under this cat fight.

Our cats are part of a set of forty-six tapestries commissioned from Goya by the future king, Charles IV. The aim is to break away from traditional battle or hunting tapestries and decorate the dining room with lively, pleasant images.

Early in his career, Goya paints numerous models for the factory. He paints with realism and vivacity, in the spirit of the late 18th-century Enlightenment. His picturesque style depicts the anecdotes of everyday life, both noble and common. For example, a fight of stray cats observed on a street corner. These cats also remind us of Goya's fascination with dark, mysterious atmospheres. A few years later, Goya becomes deaf. He then develops a disquieting universe, haunted by themes of madness and witchcraft.

Stored in the Cellar

Woven from precious materials, tapestries are considered first-rate works of art. This is not the case for the **painted models**, which are sometimes thrown away. *Cats Fighting* was rolled up and forgotten in a cellar in the 18th century. It was not until 1984 that the painting was officially attributed to Goya.

Black Cat

The **fear of** black animals, associated with the **Devil** and **witches**, has been widespread throughout Europe since the Middle Ages, and becomes more pronounced from the 16th to the 18th century. We are wary of black cats, but also of crows, dogs, chickens, roosters, goats, and black rams.

"Cats are traitors. Call them lounge tigers. Cut their tail to prevent staggers."

Gustave Flaubert, *The Dictionary of Received Ideas*

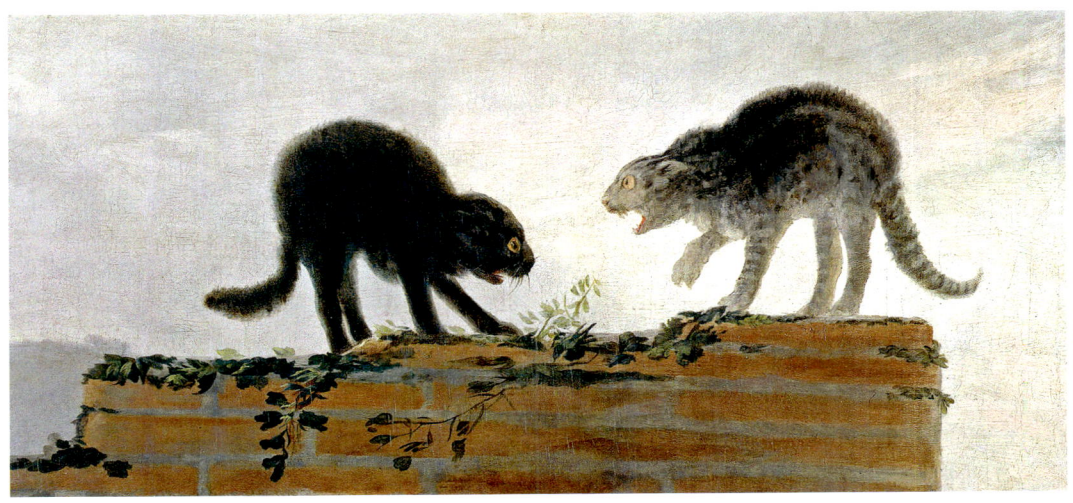

Cats Fighting
(Riña de gatos)
Francisco de Goya
1786–1787
Oil on canvas
Museo del Prado, Madrid

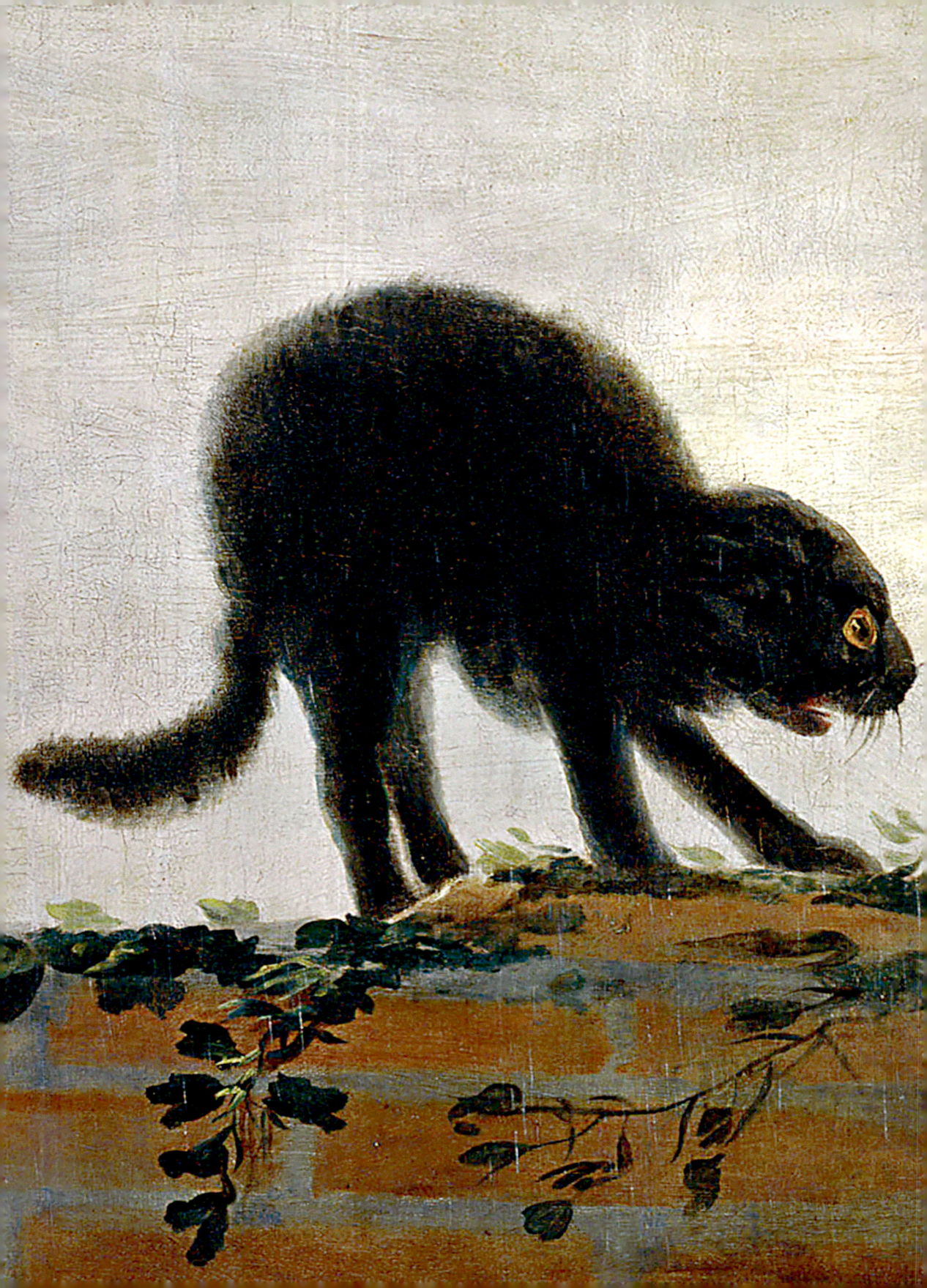

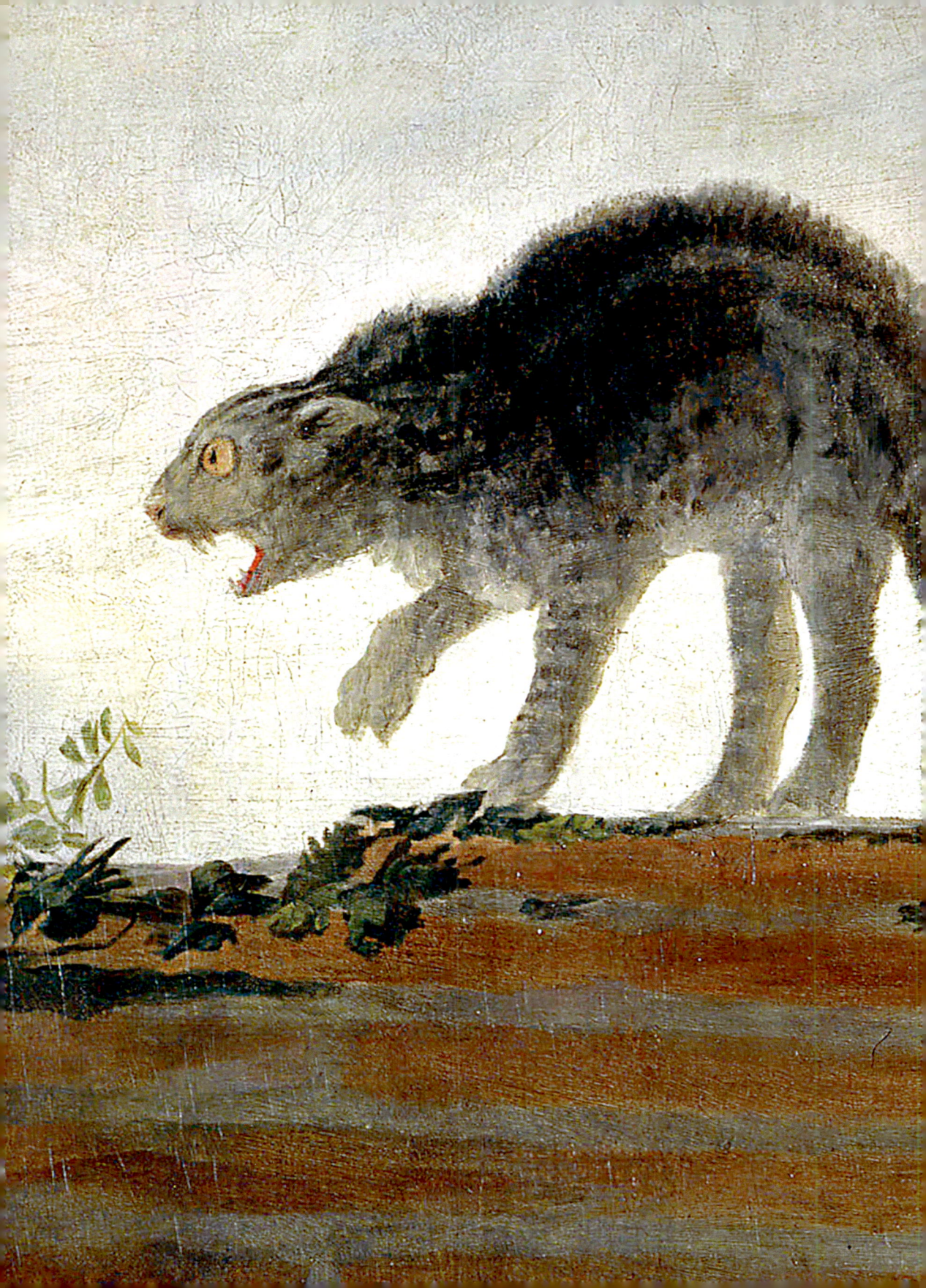

Cat; Trotting; Change to Galloping

1871–1885

One, Two, Three . . . Shoot!

Scientist **Étienne Jules Marey** invents the "photographic rifle" in 1882. The camera is mounted on a real rifle, modified to take twelve continuous shots on circular plates. He also coins the term "chronophotograph" in 1889.

KEY FIGURES
Photography and Cinema

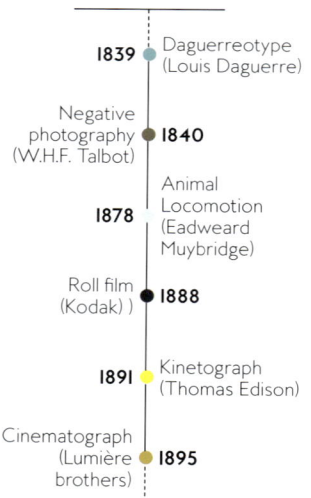

1839 — Daguerreotype (Louis Daguerre)

Negative photography (W.H.F. Talbot) — 1840

1878 — Animal Locomotion (Eadweard Muybridge)

Roll film (Kodak)) — 1888

1891 — Kinetograph (Thomas Edison)

Cinematograph (Lumière brothers) — 1895

Freeze Frames

Before the invention of cinema, the Englishman Eadweard Muybridge and the Frenchman Étienne Jules Marey both carried out research on the immobilization of movement: this is chronophotography.

Here's a tabby cat running at full speed. The movement of its light, supple run is broken down into twenty successive shots: we can see an acceleration, from a gentle trot to a dynamic gallop, during which the cat leaps twice. Its body picks itself up, then stretches as it leaps. The feline seems to fly low to the ground before landing smoothly and precisely. In reality, these twenty shots correspond to a single second of racing. The elusive, the fleeting, is frozen on film.

This cat was published by Muybridge in 1887, in his *Animal Locomotion* collection. A veritable sum: eleven volumes, four thousand photographs. A hundred or so plates show horses, while the others range from elephants to parrots, including dogs, lions, pigs, and ostriches. To our contemporary eye, these series in black and white are hardly surprising. But in 1887, they are revolutionary. This is ten years before the invention of cinema. The movement is a fantasy. As for photography, it is not widely available and is often confined to portraits and landscapes. Muybridge's images have a great impact. These are images that go beyond the limits of the human eye. They fascinate the public, from scientists to artists. What an aid to creation!

He is the first to take an interest in decomposition of movement. He begins by breaking down a horse's gallop. To do this, he has the idea of using a series of automatic cameras. Initially, there are as many cameras as there are images. The Frenchman Marey pursued the idea and, in 1882, perfected a technique for taking burst shots with a single camera.

"In my opinion, you cannot say you have thoroughly seen anything until you have got a photograph of it."
Émile Zola

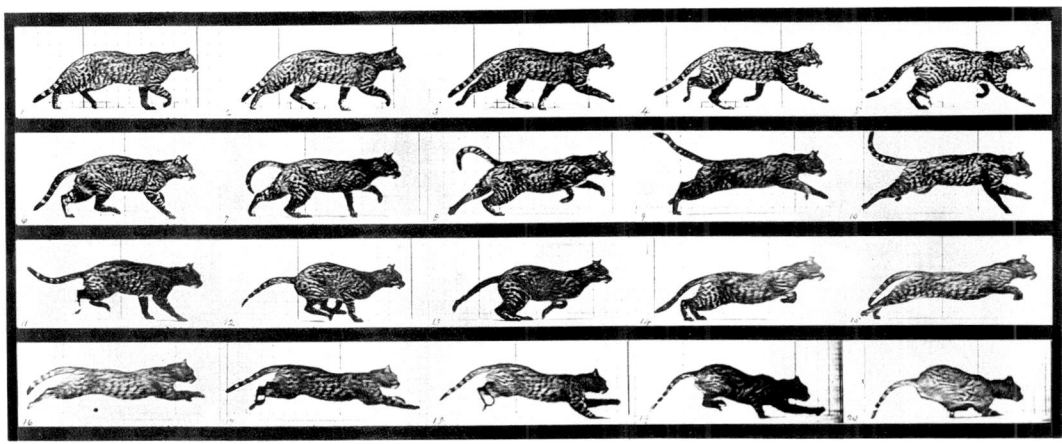

Cat; Trotting; Change to Galloping
Eadweard Muybridge
1871-1885
Collotype on white paper
Royal Academy of Arts, London

The Yellow Cat

1880

Trinket Cat

What is the École de Nancy?

École de Nancy, also called Alliance Provinciale des Industries d'Art, is formed around 1900 and combines ancient Lorraine skills like ceramics, glassmaking, and cabinetmaking. The school becomes one of the spearheads of the Art Nouveau style in France. **Majorelle, Daum** and **Gallé** are its leading representatives.

The Symbolism of Yellow

Appreciated in Eastern cultures (Turkey, Iran, India, China, etc.), **yellow** is disliked in the West from the Middle Ages to modern times. And with good reason, in the Christian tradition, the color is associated with **envy**, **lies**, and **betrayal**—in the image of Judas' cloak.

The Yellow Cat
(Le Chat jaune)
Émile Gallé
1880
Ceramic and glass paste
Musée départemental Maurice-Denis, Saint-Germain-en-Laye

A friendly cat, yellow as a lemon, stares at us with round eyes. What an unusual decoration for your living room! Between traditional ceramics and Art Nouveau objects, this cat embodies the taste of an era.

This amusing little yellow cat is a decorative object approximately thirteen inches high. It is made of ceramic and covered in a bright yellow glaze. Its two translucent green eyes are made of glass paste. The only elements painted black are the eyebrows and moustache. The drooping black eyebrows and upturned moustache are not really those of a cat. These unexpected, rather comical details make the cat look like a gentleman in the fashion of the 1880s.

It is a work by Émile Gallé. Ceramist, cabinetmaker, and glassmaker, he bridges the gap between art, science, and industry. His cat dates back to 1880, when he worked in the family business, Maison Gallé-Reinemer. Our yellow cat is not unique! Many almost identical felines are produced, and bear the monogram G. R., for Gallé-Reinemer, under their base. Some are decorated with blue or red hearts, or flowers. All are the same lemon yellow.

But why yellow? Émile Gallé's cat is in the tradition of the animal trinkets found in eastern France and Germany, but it breaks with naturalism by adopting a supple form typical of Art Nouveau and using an unexpected color. In the 18th and 19th centuries, bright yellow evoked the East. Émile Gallé was fascinated by Chinese and Japanese decorative arts. Yellow, depreciated for centuries in the West, is in fact the color of power in the Middle Kingdom.

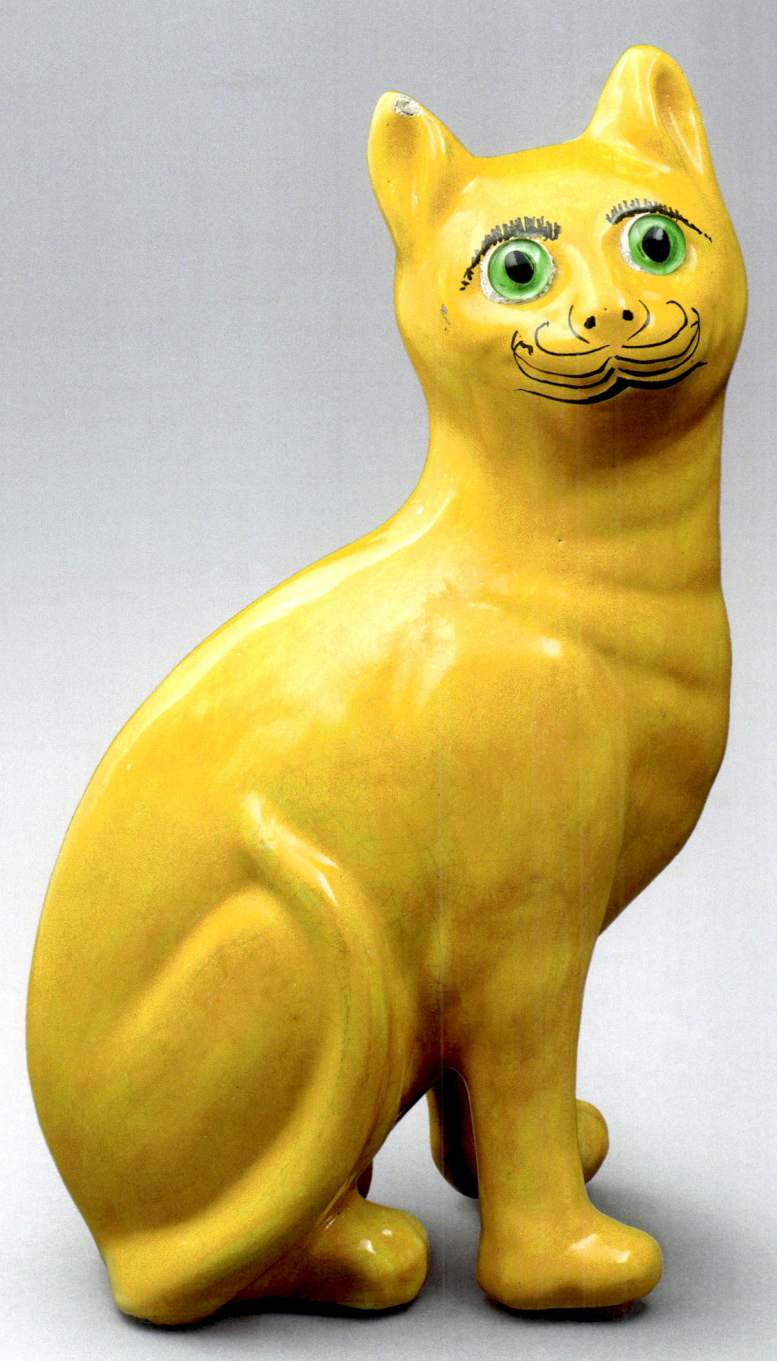

Portrait of Mr. X

Around 1910

Did You Say Naive?

This portrait has long been interpreted as that of the writer Pierre Loti. If this hypothesis seems abandoned, it's still tempting to see the author of *An Iceland Fisherman* there, among other things because of the presence of a cat.

Henri Rousseau, known as Douanier Rousseau, a naive and completely self-taught painter, describes his *Portrait of Mr. X* as a "landscape portrait." This genre, which he claims to have invented, is based on the codes of Italian Renaissance portraiture. The principle is simple: a bust figure is placed in front of a natural landscape with small trees. Beyond the horizon, a peaceful blue sky opens up. But this is a modern painting: there's a factory in the background.

In front of this landscape stand a cat and its master. They look like two frozen, inexpressive puppets. Both are painted with great frontality. The only dynamic element in the canvas is the man's raised hand, a glowing cigarette clasped between his index and middle fingers. The little tabby feline is depicted in a way that is both childlike and enigmatic: sitting on a curious red stand that puts it at his master's height. It stares at us, wide-eyed.

Although Rousseau was mocked for his clumsy style, he was admired by Vallotton and Picasso, and counted the writers Jarry, Cendrars, and Apollinaire among his friends. *Portrait of Mr. X* bears a striking resemblance to a photograph of Pierre Loti taken around 1904. The thick black moustache, the fez (Loti was passionate about Turkey and wore one at home), the high white shirt collar, and, of course, the cat all point to the writer-traveler. For Pierre Loti was a cat lover. The identity of the model remains uncertain, however. Another writer, Edmond Franck, claims to have posed for this portrait.

Why "Douanier?"

Before devoting himself to painting, Henri Rousseau worked in the inland **port** service on the Seine as a junior employee, or *gabelou*. Although some goods are taxed at the various octrois, Henri is not really a customs officer ("douanier" in French), but he adopts this nickname.

Passion for Felines

Douanier Rousseau often paints **cats**—alone, accompanied, sometimes tiny, but his preference is for larger felines. **Tigers**, **lions**, **leopards**, and **panthers** populate his imaginary jungles. Surprising for an artist whose only trips are visits to the Ménagerie at the Jardin des Plantes in Paris!

Portrait of Mr. X (Pierre Loti)
(Portrait de Monsieur X, Pierre Loti)
Henri Rousseau
Around 1910
Oil on canvas
Kunsthaus, Zurich

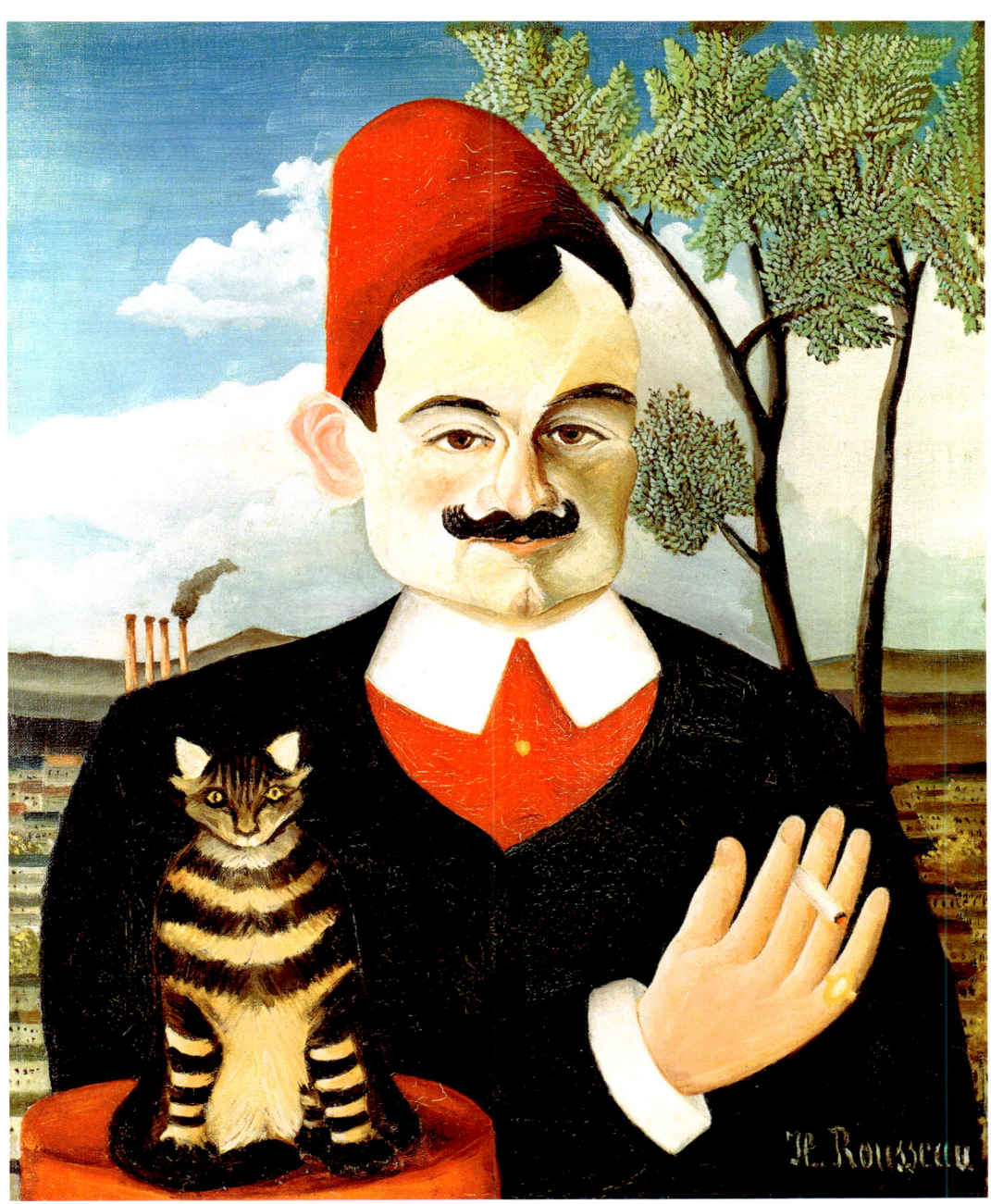

Madame Ranson with Cat

Around 1892

Tone on Tone

Madame Ranson's cat almost merges with the folds of her dress. Its presence affirms what the painter had theorized a few years earlier: painting is above all a story of lines, patterns, and colors.

In a wallpapered interior, France Ranson takes tea, dressed in a long yellow dress with puffed sleeves. Madame Ranson welcomes her husband Paul-Élie's artist friends to her Parisian studio on Boulevard du Montparnasse. At her feet, mingling with the folds of her dress, a little cat rubs its neck. Its yellow and black stripes are almost identical to the black folds of the dress, just as its little pointy ears echo the tiny shoes that protrude from the garment. Finally, its tail, raised in an arabesque, echoes the suppleness of its mistress's chignon.

Since he was eighteen, Maurice Denis has been saying: Painting is not reality. There's no point in looking for the illusion. Impressionism is totally outdated. On the contrary, painting is a pure, poetic, and symbolic art. The painter intertwines lines and colors. In 1890 he writes: "Remember that a painting—before being a warhorse, a naked woman, or some anecdote—is essentially a flat surface covered with colors in a certain assembled order."

Maurice Denis and his fellow Nabis wish to renew painting. The young painters are inspired by Japanese art. They abandon traditional perspective and work with colors in a flat area, like a stencil. We notice that the cat and its mistress seem to float in front of the tapestry, casting no shadows.

Who Are the Nabis?

Sérusier, **Bonnard**, **Denis**, **Ranson**, **Vuillard**, **Roussel**, and **Vallotton** are young painters with a keen interest in literature and esoteric texts. They call themselves the Nabis ("prophets" in Hebrew). Between 1888 and 1890, they develop a decorative, Japanese style that breaks with the illusion of reality.

Ambient Japonisme

Between 1860 and 1890, Japonisme reaches its peak in Europe. Artists, writers, collectors . . . everyone is fascinated by objects from the Land of the Rising Sun, draws inspiration from them, or collects them. This is the case of **Monet**, **Van Gogh**, **Degas**, **Denis**, **Loti**, **Zola**, and **Proust**, to name a few.

Madame Ranson with Cat
(Portrait de Madame Ranson au chat)
Maurice Denis
Around 1892
Oil on canvas
Musée départemental Maurice-Denis, Saint-Germain-en-Laye

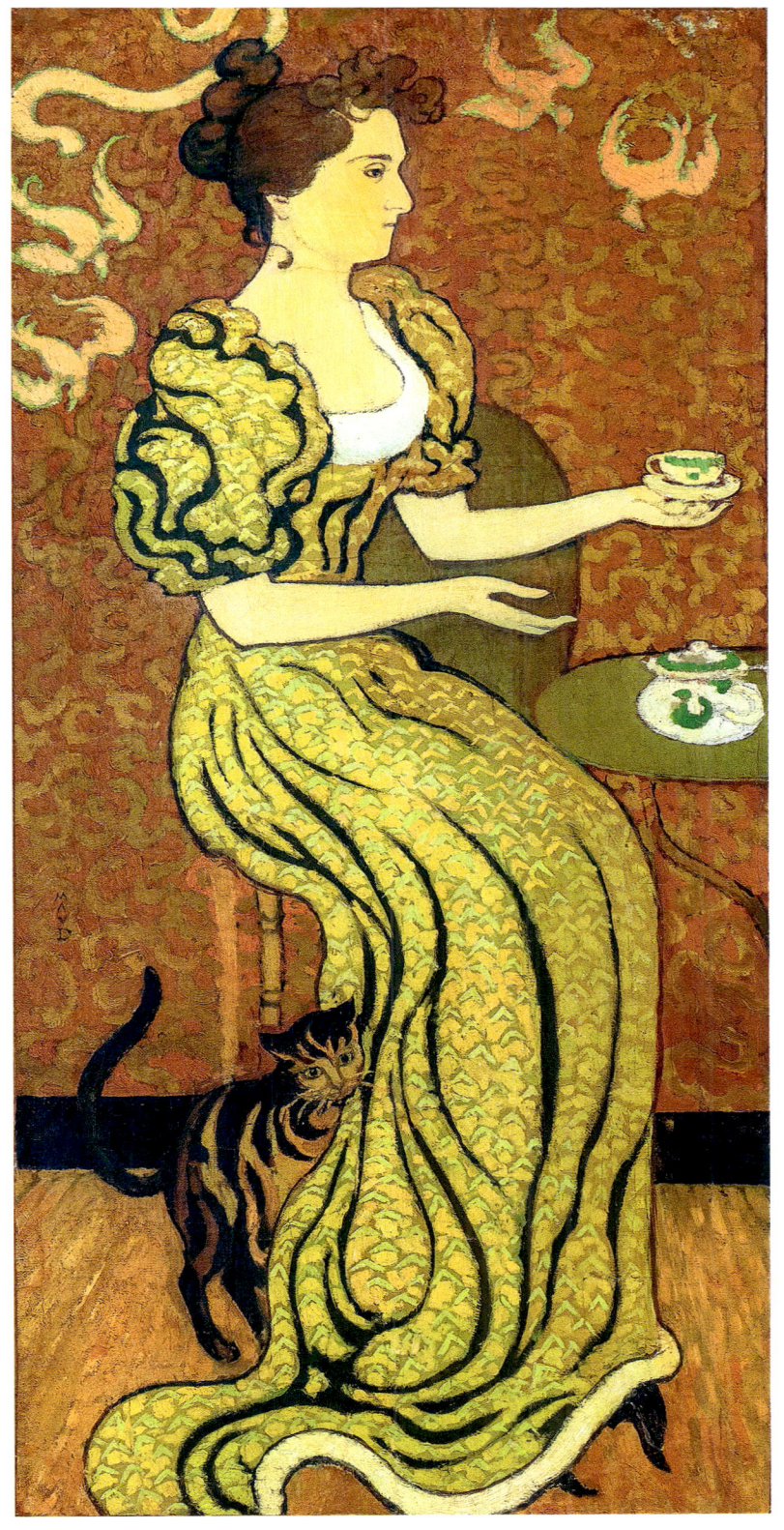

Eiaha Ohipa

1896

Island Cat

When he arrives in Tahiti in 1891, Gauguin is struck by the colors, the light, the bodies . . . and the silence, an omnipresent silence that will invade him.

In 1895, he returns to Tahiti after two years of personal and artistic failure. He paints melancholic and mysterious characters, like these two Tahitians. The house is that of Gauguin himself, in Punaauia. It is the setting for several of his compositions.

The man, seated and motionless, is dressed in a white loincloth. He smokes tobacco nonchalantly. A heavy gold ring hangs from his ear, while flowers adorn his long hair. He places his hand on the knee of the woman, dressed in a blue and yellow sarong. At their side, a white cat sleeps, curled up in a ball. Outside, a dog keeps watch. The two Tahitians do not move, do not speak, and look enigmatically at the viewer.

The cat recalls the man's loincloth. Its presence reinforces the atmosphere of silence and indolence. The purring feline is associated with interior space and sleep. "Don't work," says Gauguin in Tahitian. On the contrary, the dog is the link with the outside world: light, color, and movement.

The artist is fascinated by the graceful, androgynous Polynesian bodies, by their matte, coppery skin. Gauguin wants to see primitive purity in them. He is obsessed . He often depicts them in pairs. He studies the postures of these silent, statue-like figures, reusing them from work to work. In 1901, we find our two characters in *And the Gold of Their Bodies*. He combines his observation with his memory of Greek sculptures and Egyptian bas-reliefs. These massive figures, their faces treated like masks, will strongly influence the young Pablo Picasso. As for the arabesque patterns (cat, flowers, sarong, gate), they exude a decorative power that will interest Henri Matisse, among others.

Cats in Oceania

Cats are introduced to Oceania and Australia by European settlers in the 18th century. On Gauguin's canvases, we come across several. Two small, white cats are depicted in the foreground of the large frieze *Where Do We Come From? What Are We? Where Are We Going?*

KEY FIGURES
Gauguin the Traveler

1891 — First stay in Tahiti

Back to Paris to exhibit — 1893

1894 — Stay in Brittany

Back to Tahiti — 1895

1901 — Settling in the Marquesas (Atuona, Hiva Oa island)

Death of Gauguin in Atuona — 1903

Eiaha Ohipa (Don't Work)
Eiaha Ohipa (Ne travaille pas)
Paul Gauguin
1896
Oil on canvas
Pushkin Museum, Moscow

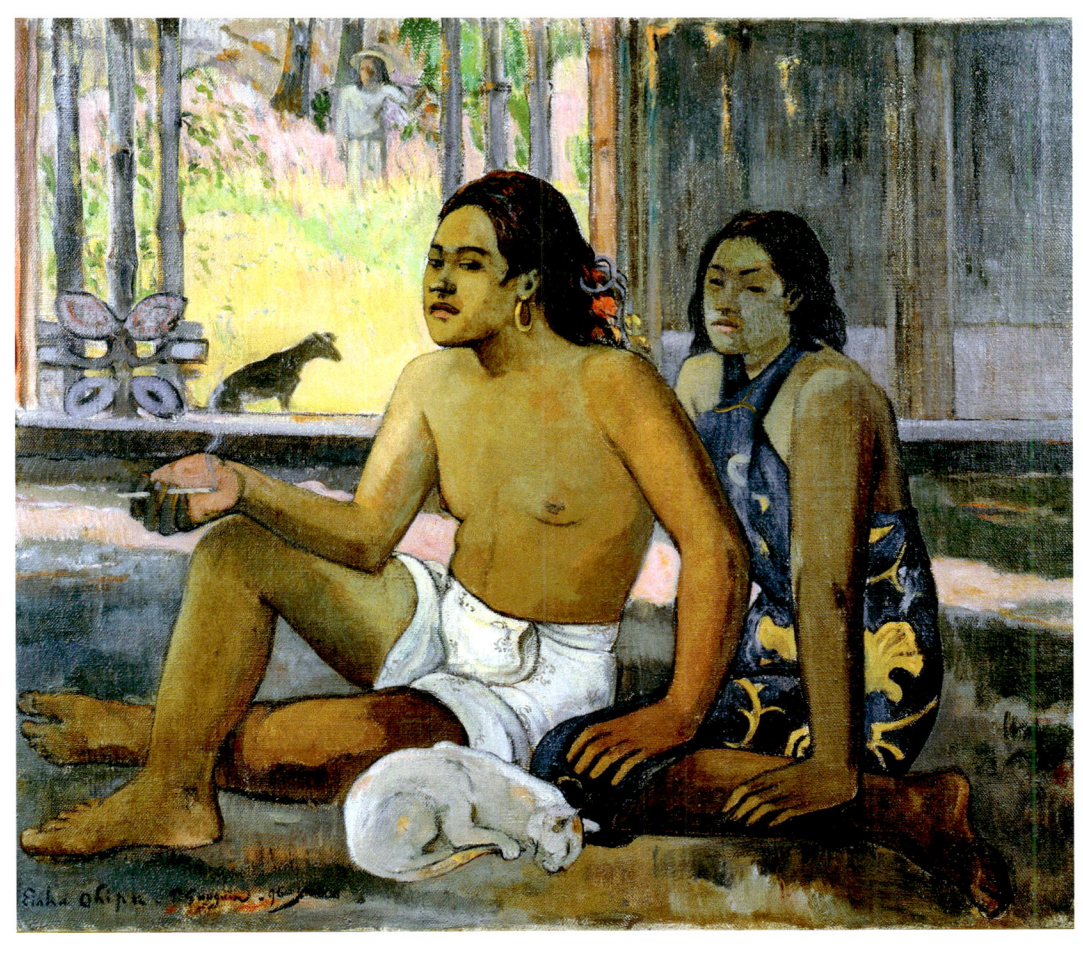

"Always this silence. I understand why these people can remain seated for hours, days at a time, without saying a word."

Paul Gauguin

Laziness

1896

At the Foot of the Bed

Better a Cat!

When **Vallotton** married, his wife was a widow with three children aged seven, nine, and twelve. He didn't like them very much, writing in a letter to the painter **Vuillard**: "I prefer cats even better than children, because you can kick them off a table."

Vallotton is a Swiss artist with a Protestant background. He has a taste for line, constraint, and a job well done. Fascinated by female nudes and Japanese prints, he practices wood engraving with virtuosity.

A naked woman, languid on her bed, lounges. Lying on her stomach, she turns her head to look at her approaching cat. The cat begs for a caress. It stands up on its paws to reach his mistress. With her fingertips, the woman caresses the top of its head, between the ears. This masterly black-and-white engraving is entitled *Laziness*. We can feel the softness of the curvaceous body. Feminine lines marry those of the cushions. The nonchalant arm extends into the supple body of the feline. The cat has long been associated with femininity, eroticism, and laziness. This association seems to grow stronger in the 19th century, becoming a favorite subject of the Symbolists and the Nabis, a group to which Vallotton belongs.

This small etching bears witness to the artist's virtuosity in working with line and solid colors. The whiteness of the figures, framed by a thick black outline, contrasts with the motifs of the blankets and cushions. Vallotton plays with checks, dots, curves, and zigzags. In his compositions, he also plays with framing. He uses high angles, low angles, and cropped figures. The woman is seen from above, her feet sticking out of the frame. Vallotton is an avid photographer. He will buy his first Kodak three years later, in 1899, and use it for his female nudes.

A jack-of-all-trades, his engravings are a great success. He deals with everything: a riot in the street, a downpour that causes umbrellas to open, a landscape, the world's fair, department stores, scenes of couples or female intimacy, and much more.

"God made the cat in order that man might have the pleasure of caressing the tiger."
Victor Hugo

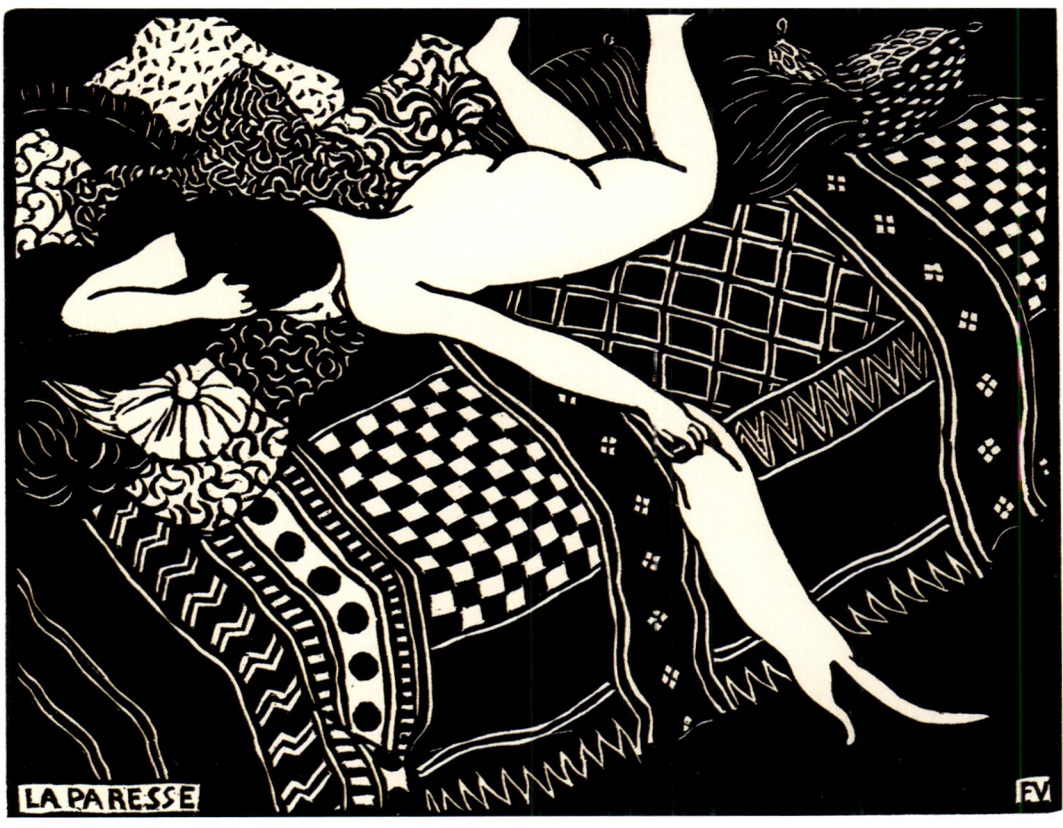

Laziness
(La paresse)
Félix Vallotton
1896
Ink on paper
Musée d'Art et d'Histoire, Geneva

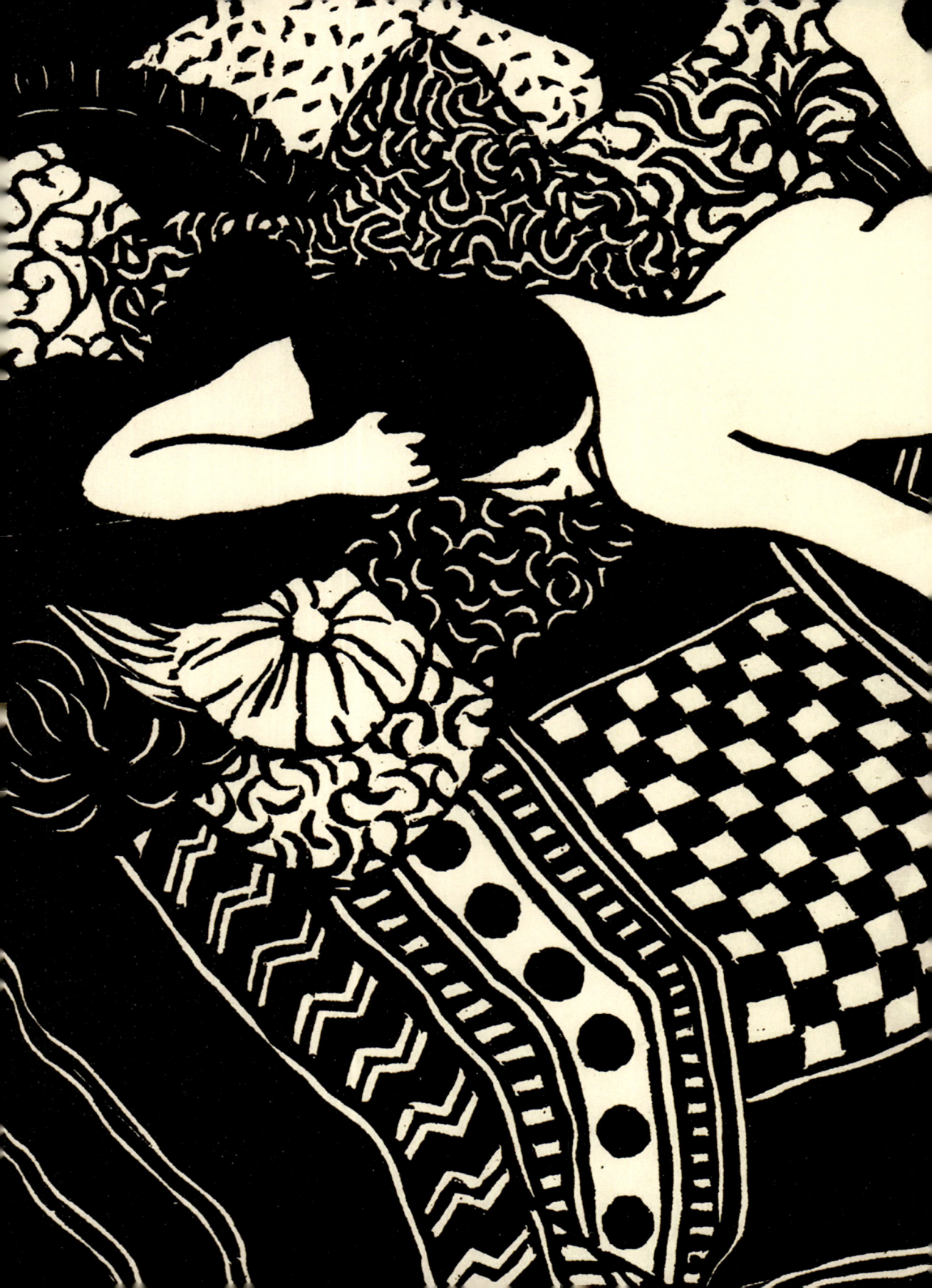

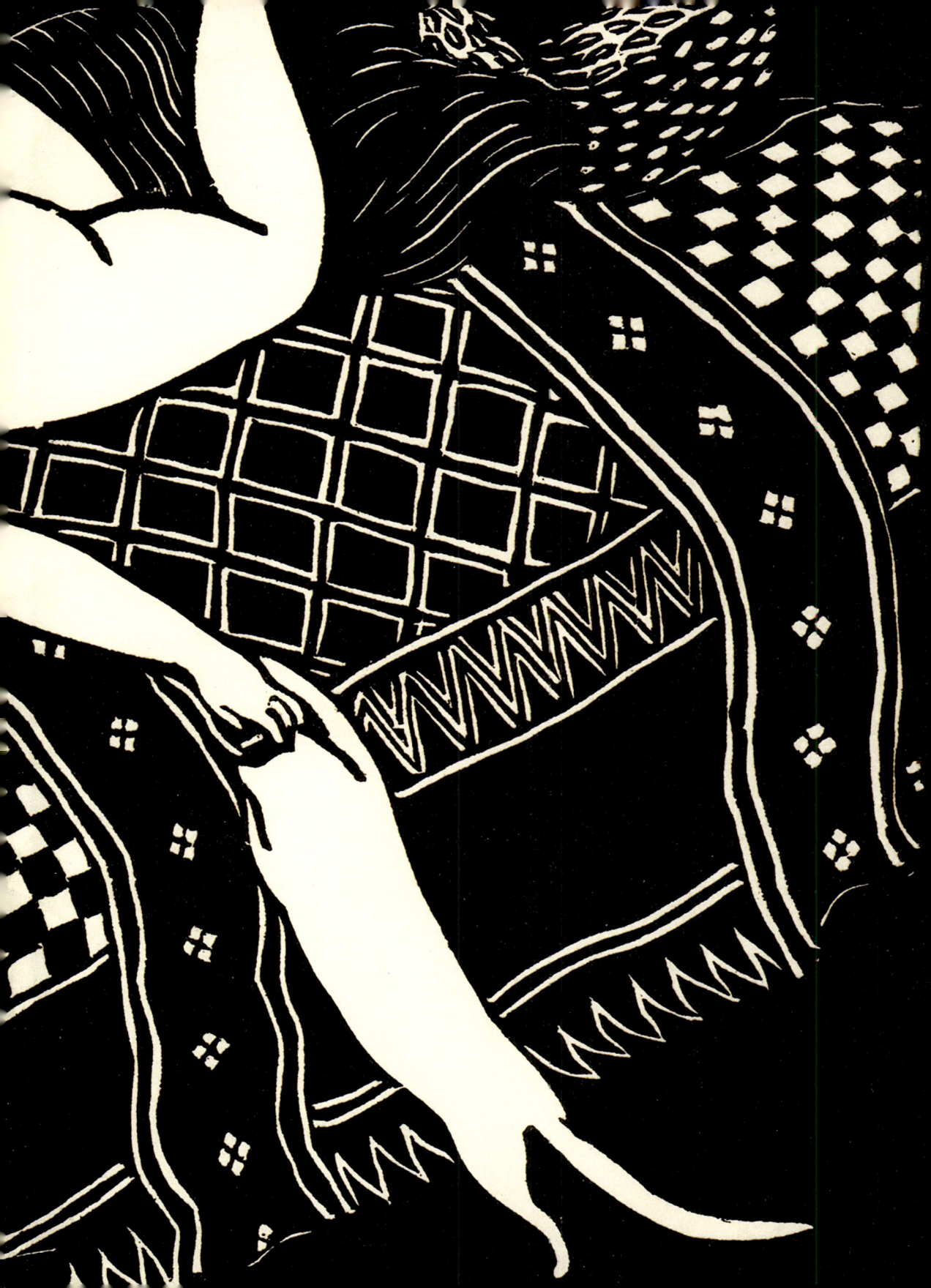

Paris through the Window

1913

Strange Cat

When Chagall arrived in Paris, he discovers the City of Light and the avant-garde. He is fascinated by Matisse's Fauvism and Picasso's Cubism.

Chagall depicts himself in an apartment, like a Janus-faced man. One looks out, perhaps towards his native Russia. The other turns to the open window. He admires a Parisian view: small buildings huddled at the foot of the Eiffel Tower. A couple in love (a reminder of his fiancée, Bella, who stayed behind in Russia) float at the foot of the Iron Lady, while a parachutist hovers near its summit. A train passes upside down. On the windowsill stands a curious cat with the head of a man.

Animals run through all of Chagall's work. The most recurrent are those of his youth in Vitebsk, Belarus. He paints fish, a memory of his father who worked in a herring depot, but above all, roosters, goats, and donkeys, the gentle, harmless animals from the farm of his childhood, memories of a poor and happy rural Russia. The cat is different. In fact, it's very rare in Chagall's work. But the context is special: we're in Paris, and the cat goes hand in hand with Parisian artists and intellectuals.

Chagall's animals have a double meaning. In the Hasidic Jewish tradition in which he grew up, the animal often merges with the human. It is therefore never to be taken at face value; it is a way of representing ourselves. Nocturnal, solitary, and a bit of a wanderer, the cat reflects the bohemian life the young painter is discovering.

The cat looks towards the Eiffel Tower: a symbol of modern life and a nod to Chagall's friend Robert Delaunay, whose dynamic and colorful Cubism strongly influenced him. The fragmented aspect of Cubism meets his Russian taste for bright, cheerful colors.

The Little Parachutist

Is the cat looking at the **Eiffel Tower** or at the little **parachutist** who jumps from it? Characters defying the laws of gravity appear frequently in Chagall's work. In 1910, parachuting was in its infancy, and on February 4, 1912, in Paris, an over-confident inventor, **François Reichelt**, soared in a suit of his own making from the top of the Eiffel Tower. The jump was fatal and made the headlines.

Marc Chagall's Symbolic Bestiary

———

The rooster: sacrifice in Judaism, renewal, vitality
The goat: innocence, tenderness, nursery rhymes, Jewish holidays, scapegoats
The donkey: docility, tenderness, happiness
The cow: childhood, rural Russia
The fish: father of the artist, pleasure, mobility, passing time

"I chose painting because it . . . seemed to me like a window through which I could have taken flight toward another world."
Marc Chagall

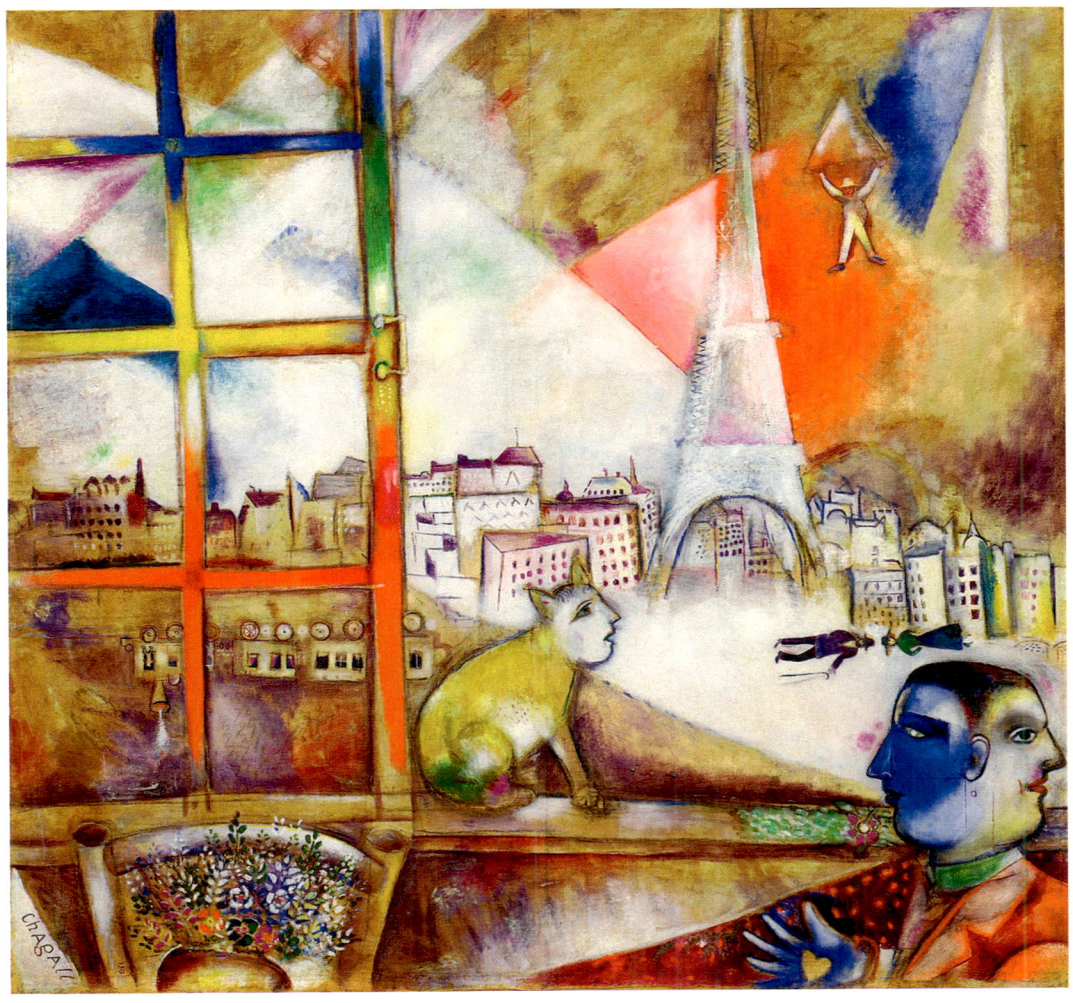

Paris through the Window
(Paris par la fenêtre)
Marc Chagall
1913
Oil on canvas
Solomon R. Guggenheim Museum,
New York

Our Cat Ulysses and Martine's Shadow

Happy Who Like Ulysses . . .

Du Bellay's Famous Sonnet

Happy the traveler
who like Ulysses
or like the hero who
brought home the Fleece
returns at last,
experienced and wise,
to spend among his
people his last years!

Feline Muses

———

Sensual, mysterious,
contemplative . . .
cats inspire many
photographers. Famous
feline photographers
include **Brassaï**, **André
Kertész**, **Jacques-Henri
Lartigue**, **Dora Maar**, and
Willy Ronis.

*Our Cat Ulysses and Martine's
Shadow*
(*Notre chat Ulysse et l'ombre
de Martine*)
Henri Cartier-Bresson
1989
Gelatin silver print
Private collection

Surrealist, great reporter, co-founder of Magnum agency, Henri Cartier-Bresson is nicknamed the "Eye of the Century." For a man who has traveled all his life, it's hardly surprising that he calls his cat Ulysses!

Ulysses, the cat of Cartier-Bresson and his second wife, photographer Martine Franck, basks on an armchair. The black tomcat with white paws lies in full light. The shadows of his profile and that of his mistress, out of frame, stand out with elegance and sharpness. The photograph is in black and white. Cartier-Bresson does not appreciate color, working with it only rarely and out of obligation. He works on balance: black and white, straight and curved, light and shadow.

Ulysses' curves echo the shape and profile of the chair. Its legs respond to the line of the bust of Martine and the strips of the ground in the background. This skillful and meticulous composition is characteristic of the man who originally wanted to become a painter.

The photograph dates from 1989. Cartier-Bresson is then eighty-one years old. He has crossed eras, styles, and countries. He has officially stopped photographing, but still carries his trusty Leica in his pocket.

The poetic randomness of the shadows on the armchair recalls the Surrealist aesthetic of the 1930s: at the age of twenty, the shy Cartier-Bresson attended meetings of the Surrealist group. The sweet silence of the dozing feline, on the other hand, takes us back to his last Asian travels: after a long stay in Japan in 1965, he takes a more relaxed approach to photography and discovers a passion for Zen Buddhism. In retirement, the photographer visits museums, draws, and occasionally takes pictures: intimate, contemplative photographs, just for fun. Just like that of Ulysses.

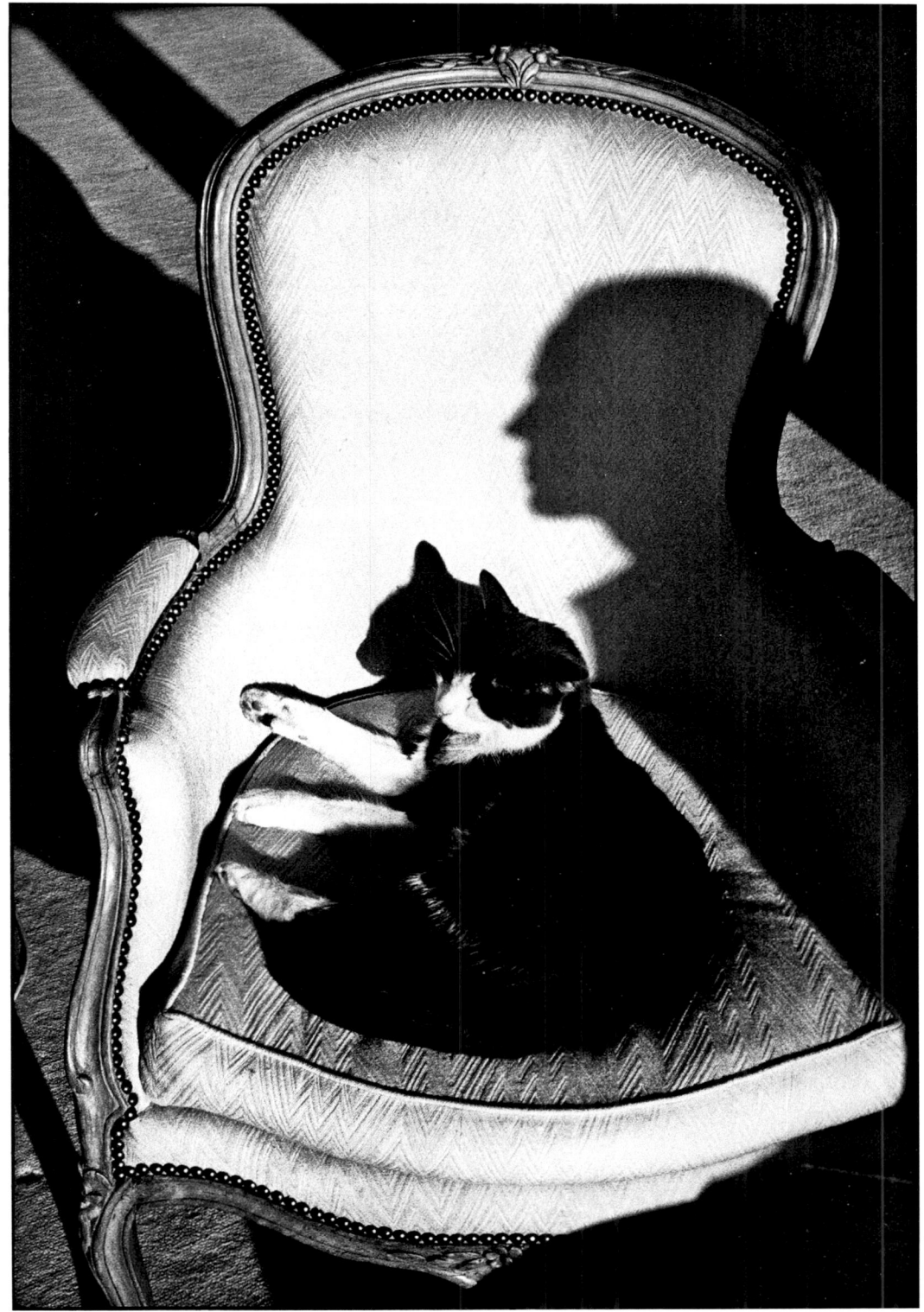

Cat on a Clothesline

1994-2001

KEY FIGURES
Koons' Bestiary

1979	*Inflatable Flower and Bunny*
Rabbit	1986
1988	*Michael Jackson and Bubbles*
Puppy	1992
1994-2000	*Balloon Dog*
Dolphin	2007-2013

Neo-Pop Kitten

Jeff Koons cultivates kitsch and provocation. He is certainly among the most controversial artist of the turn of the century. His most popular works are inflatable rabbits and dogs. His childlike cat is part of the so-called hyperpop aesthetic.

A little cat hangs in a sock and stares at us. It doesn't look like a real cat, but a plastic toy. Its representation is simplified; its colors uniform. The cat is held in place by two clothespins while two large fanciful daisies, one blue and one pink, frame the sculpture.

Fun, simple, and neon, the gadgets and products of consumer society are an inexhaustible source of inspiration. Koons says he wonders about their glorification. He plays with this very large format: our cat in his sock is over ten feet tall. A star of calendars, postcards, and the Internet, the cat—and especially the kitten—became popular in homes in the late 20th and early 21st centuries. It becomes the cutest animal par excellence. Cuddly, endearing, funny . . . it has lost the connotations of previous centuries.

This cat sculpture is part of a series initiated in 1994 and entitled *Celebration*. After exhibiting industrial objects in the 1980s, Koons works on their monumental, ultra-colorful serial reproduction. *Cat on a Clothesline* exists in five copies, each in a different color.

Koons' works skillfully blend artistic references and popular culture. Accessible to all, they seem to be designed as a by-product even though they are hardly accessible. A paradox skillfully cultivated by the artist, who is also an excellent businessman.

Cat on a Clothesline
Jeff Koons
1994-2001
Polyethylene
Collection of the artist

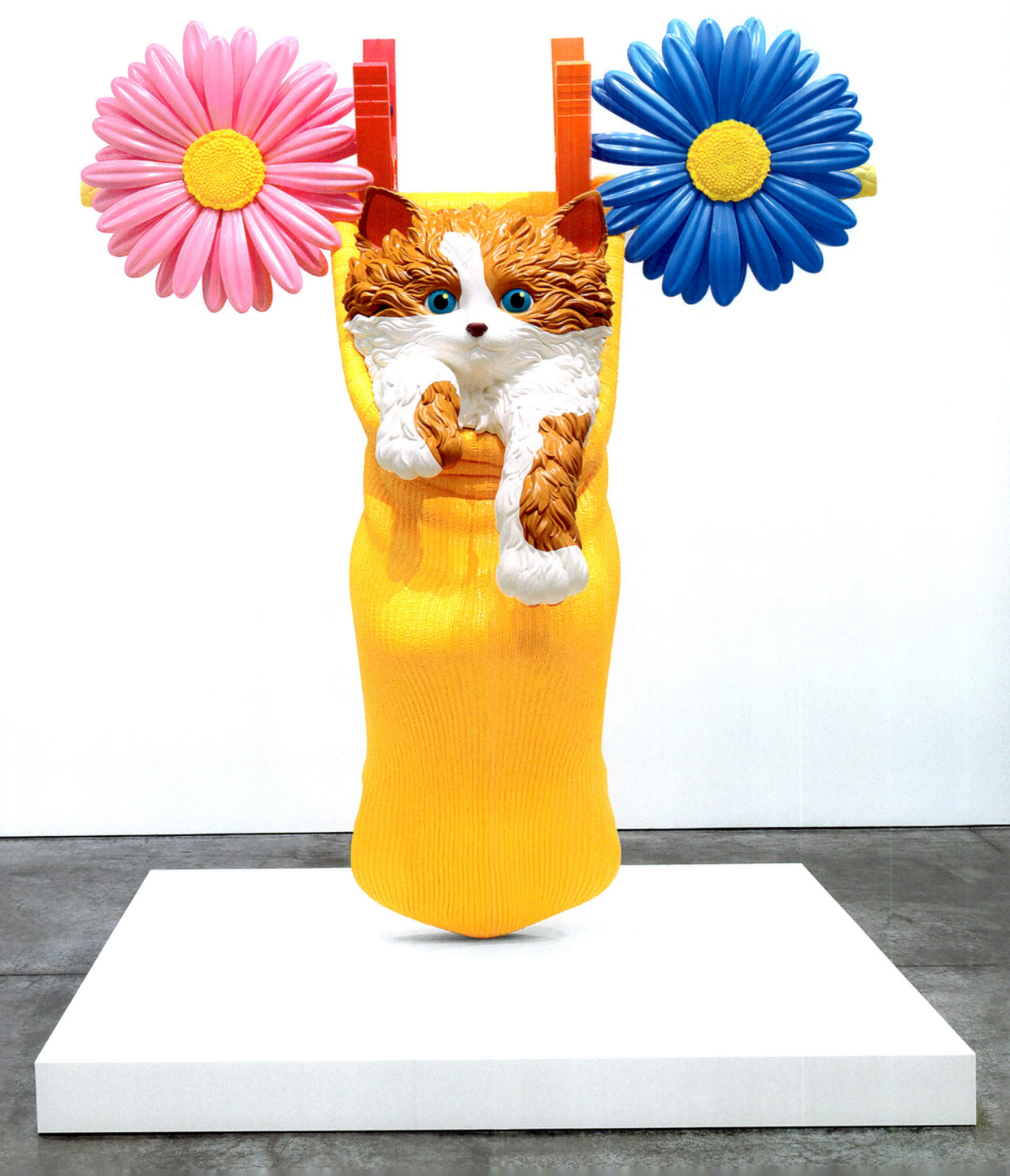

Table of Illustrations

THE UNEXPECTED

Credits

Cats in Art: From Prehistoric to Neo-Pop Masterpieces

Author
Alix Paré

U.S. Edition Team

Publisher and Creative Director
Ilona Oppenheim

Art Director and Cover Design
Jefferson Quintana

Typesetter
Morgane Leoni

Editorial Director
Lisa McGuinness

Editor
Jessica Faroy

Printed and bound in China by Artron Art Co., Ltd.

Cats in Art: From Prehistoric to Neo-Pop Masterpieces was first published in the United States by Tra Publishing in 2024. © Hachette Livre (Editions du Chêne), 2020.

All rights reserved. No part of this book may be reproduced or transmitted in any form or by any means (electronic or mechanical, including photocopying, recording or any information retrieval system) without permission in writing from the publisher.

ISBN: 978-1-962098-05-2

Cats in Art: From Prehistoric to Neo-Pop Masterpieces is printed on Forest Stewardship Council-certified paper from well-managed forests.

Tra Publishing is committed to sustainability in its materials and practices.

Tra Publishing
245 NE 37th Street
Miami, FL 33137
trapublishing.com

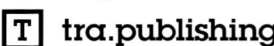

3 4 5 6 7 8 9 10